D1493419

Dolphins

Dolphins

Antony Alpers

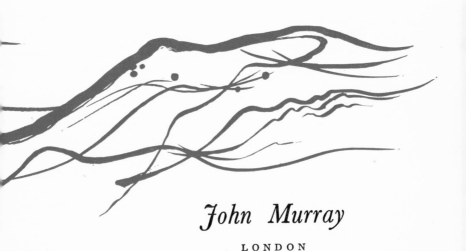

John Murray

LONDON

BY THE SAME AUTHOR

Katherine Mansfield: a biography

(JONATHAN CAPE)

First edition 1960
Second edition 1963
Reprinted 1963

© ANTONY ALPERS 1960, 1963

Printed in Great Britain
Butler & Tanner Ltd, Frome and London

To Merrill Moore, who suggested it
to A. R. D. Fairburn and W. D'Arcy Cresswell
who also would have liked to read it
and to T. H. Scott, who made it possible
'remembering their gentle friendship'

ἀρετὴ δὲ καὶ ὀλλυμένοισιν ὀπηδεῖ καὶ κράτος,
οὐδ' ἤσχυναν ἐὸν κλέος οὐδὲ θανόντες

Contents

✿   ✿   ✿   ✿

The jacket, title-page drawing, dolphin rule and line illustrations were designed by Erik Thorn. The photographs of Opononi are all the work of Spencer Hill. Plates: 7–12, Frank Essapian; 1, Staatliche Antikensammlungen, Munich, photo by Prof. Dr Max Hirmer; 2, courtesy, Museum of Fine Arts, Boston; 3–6, British Museum, photos by Larkin Bros.

Illustrations

Foreword

This book is an enlarged version of its predecessor *A Book of Dolphins*, published in 1960. Of its three parts, the first and last stand much as they were, but the middle or biological section has been entirely recast. There is also now a full list of references, and a chronological appendix, *Delphinology*.

I think it will help the reader to know how the book reached its present form. As I explained in the preface to the first edition, the book had its origins in the early summer of 1956, when the dolphinet known as 'Opo' was playing with the bathers and children at Opononi, north of Auckland. My friend the American poet and psychiatrist Merrill Moore, who was visiting New Zealand, stopped me in the street in Auckland and urged me to write a short book for children 'about that dolphin', and I rashly promised him I would. I had not then read any zoology or animal psychology and knew nothing of ancient natural history; and as soon as I set to work, my subject, with one flick of her graceful tail, swam off into those deeper waters, leaving me no choice but to follow. I found, however, as I read the classical writers, that wherever dolphins have chosen to make human acquaintance, children have always been accorded first rights to their friendship. I therefore tried to preserve that principle in *A Book of Dolphins*, and have done the same in this longer and more scientific version; and I hope the pages following will now give pleasure to readers of any age.

In its process of growth the book received the generous

help of many persons in New Zealand and the United States. This will be obvious from the text, and their kindness has already been acknowledged in the earlier editions, but I would like to mention again three of those who helped from the beginning. First, F. G. Wood, Jr, Director of Exhibits at Marine Studios, Marineland, Florida, who sent me many scientific papers, patiently answered many questions, and read two versions of the manuscript, all for the sake of adding, as he said, 'to the goodness and glory of dolphins everywhere'. Second, Andrew Packard, formerly lecturer in zoology at the University of Auckland, who with equal patience and generosity guided my first studies in zoology, and also read the manuscript. Third, the late Dr T. H. Scott, head of the Psychology Department of the same university, who made me see what I had really undertaken, and caused me to enlarge the early drafts and attempt a proper account of dolphin behaviour. It was these three who made possible the first version of the book.

A Book of Dolphins was the first attempt at a full account of the dolphin drawing on modern and ancient sources. But by the end of 1960, when it was published, scientific studies of the animal were in full swing. Indeed, two other books were already being written by American scientists engaged in dolphin research, which have since appeared. It was obvious that for my second edition I would have to extend the work still further; and with much encouragement and help from Dr W. N. Kellogg, Professor of Experimental Psychology at the Florida State University, and the author of one of those books, I did so.

The new scientific work referred to is all described in Part II of this book. Foremost among it was the research on dolphin echo-location done by Dr Kellogg himself, described in his *Porpoises and Sonar* and summarised here on pages 128–131. Complementing this work was that on the anatomy and function of the cetacean ear done at the British Museum (Natural History) by Dr F. C. Fraser and P. E. Purves, reported at a discussion meeting of the Royal Society in 1959 and now described to the best of my ability on pages 133–135. In 1960 Max O. Kramer published his findings on how the dolphin's skin reduces friction drag (page 64), and Dr John C. Lilly of the Virgin Islands made world headlines with his experiments on the dolphin brain (page 105), which he also has described in his book, *Man and Dolphin*. At the end of 1960 Andrew A. Fejer and Richard H. Backus published their paper on the hydrodynamics of dolphin bow-riding, which probably has settled that teasing controversy (page 68). At this time, too, Sir James Gray, of Cambridge University, author of *How Animals Move*, was kind enough to answer my questions on dolphin locomotion (page 73); and material for the new section on commensal fishing of men and dolphins fell into place from various sources. Finally, the revised Part II was read in Florida and Naples by Forrest Wood and Andrew Packard with such scrupulous care that I scarcely know how to thank them. I can only say that any merits which this section may now possess in the eyes of a biologist are largely owed to the pains they took.

A word about the way the book is written. Feeling it right that I should keep the youthful reader always in mind, I have set myself a double aim: on the one hand to write no paragraph that an intelligent young citizen of the modern world might not understand, and on the

other to meet as far as possible the requirements of
scientific statement; to combine, that is, the aim of giving
pleasure with the aim of being exact, while not forgetting
what is owed to the poetic vision of the myth and to
ancient natural history. This has involved some juggling
with the language in places (which I leave zoologists to
notice) but I see no essential conflict here. For there is
surely a natural harmony uniting *all* of this material, both
the science and the legend; a harmony which the dolphins
themselves express most wonderfully in the sheer perfection of their form and skill and thrift of energy.

And a word on what the book is *not*. It is not the
scientific treatise on the Delphinidae that must some day
be written by a trained zoologist. Such a book – the
successor to Norman and Fraser's, now twenty-five years
old – would eschew the lighthearted play with legend
that I have indulged in at times and deal exhaustively and
comparatively with all the species; it would perhaps compare the dolphins' adaptations with those of the larger
whales and the other 're-entrants', the seals and the
manatees, and it might also investigate the reason for
dolphin strandings, one of the many outstanding mysteries
of their behaviour. I hope that such a book will be written
soon.*

         o   o   o   o

Acknowledgment is gratefully made to the following
publishers and authors for permission to publish extracts
used (of which fuller details will be found in the References): William Heinemann Ltd, proprietors of the Loeb
Classical Library, for passages from Pliny's *Natural History*,

* Professor E. J. Slijper's *Whales*, now available in English, has
filled this need in every way.

Oppian's *Halieutica*, Aelian's *On the Characteristics of Animals*, and short extracts from Athenaios and Pausanias; the Clarendon Press, Oxford, for extracts from Sir D'Arcy Thompson's translation of Aristotle's *History of Animals*; Mr Patrick Leigh Fermor and John Murray (Publishers) Ltd, for an extract from *Mani: Travels in the Southern Peloponnese*; Mr Adrian Hayter and Hodder and Stoughton Ltd, for a passage from *Sheila in the Wind*; Mr Conor O Brien and Rupert Hart-Davis Ltd, for an excerpt from *Across Three Oceans*; Angus and Robertson Ltd, for extracts from W. J. Dakin's *Whalemen Adventurers*; Dr F. Bruce Lamb and *Natural History* magazine for extracts from 'The Fisherman's Porpoise'; the same magazine for the anonymous account of a dolphin 'rescue' of a human being; Lady Grimble and John Murray (Publishers) Ltd for passages from *A Pattern of Islands* by Sir Arthur Grimble; and Mr Piwai Toi and the New Zealand Department of Maori Affairs for passages from Mr Toi's article in *Te Ao Hou*.

On page 23, in Pliny's story of the dolphin of the Lucrine Lake, the text is that of William Colenso. For the rendering of Pliny the Younger's letter to Caninius I must take responsibility myself.

A. A.

Auckland, New Zealand
June, 1962

DOLPHINS IN ANTIQUITY

*Diviner than the dolphin is nothing yet created;
for indeed they were aforetime men and lived in
cities along with mortals, but by the devising of
Dionysos they exchanged the land for the sea and
put on the form of fishes.*

OPPIAN: *Halieutica*

IT HAPPENED FIRST BY THE SHORES of the Mediterranean Sea, at the Roman colonial town of Hippo (which is now called Bizerta) beside an estuary on the northern coast of Africa, not far from Tunis. That was nearly two thousand years ago. Then it happened again, at the little township of Opononi, which is just inside the mouth of the Hokianga Harbour on the northern coast of New Zealand. That was in 1956.

A dolphin, friendly and gentle, came to the beach and played with the children swimming there. As at Hippo, soon after the time of Christ, so at Opononi in 1956: the dolphin lived in the sea, as free as any wild animal or bird, and no one could have made it do anything it did not want to; but it came and played, and went away, and came of its own free will again.

At Opononi the dolphin played with a beach ball, and it liked to have its sides scratched with an oar. The dolphin at Hippo also let people handle it, and it let one boy take rides on its back. There was a child who rode on the dolphin at Opononi too, and at both places many people came from miles around to see the marvel – a wild creature from the sea making friends with children and men, and sporting about with such evident enjoyment of their company that no one could believe it was a fish. Of course they were right: a dolphin is not a fish. But that is something we shall come to later.

If anything exactly like this happened anywhere else, in all the centuries between the dolphin at Hippo and the one at Opononi, the world does not seem to have heard about it. All the well-known stories of dolphin friendships – both the obvious fables and those that appear to be true accounts – come from Greek and Roman times, and most of these concern a friendship with a single boy. Of a dolphin becoming friendly with many humans and entering the society of a crowd, enjoying being touched and scratched and ridden on and returning for more, there seems to be no other instance after Hippo until we come to Opononi in 1956. Certainly the people at Opononi felt at the time as if they were seeing something that had never been seen before.

It was the same at Hippo. And yet encounters with dolphins seem to have been relatively common in classical times. The Greeks and the Romans, even though they had far less opportunity than we have to hear of things that happened at another place or another time, were evidently much better acquainted with dolphins than we are today. In some Greek cities, dolphins on coins were as familiar as lions and eagles are to us, and in classical literature there are more stories about dolphins and boys, or dolphins and men, than are to be found in all the books that have been written and printed since.

There must be some reason for this. The Greeks, of course, lived close to the sea and it played a great part in their lives; but that is just as true of their descendants over the intervening centuries, and of many other coastal peoples who live by the warm or temperate waters where dolphins are found. It would seem that the Greeks – and the Romans following their example – had a special affection for the dolphin because of his character. Much as we have feeling for some wild animals and not for others, so evidently did the Greeks and the Romans regard the dolphins around their coasts.

∘   ∘   ∘   ∘

At the beginning of all the stories about dolphins is the legend of how they were created – a legend which shows that the Greeks knew very well there was something different about dolphins, and that although they lived in the sea they were not the same as fish, but were in some way more like humans.

It was said that Dionysos, the god of wine and frenzy (whom the Romans later called Bacchus), engaged a vessel to take him from the island of Ikaria to the island of Naxos; but the sailors were a crew of pirates and, not knowing that he was a god, they formed a plot to abduct him. Sailing past Naxos they made for Asia, where they intended to sell him as a slave. When he realised what they were doing he called on his magical powers. He changed the oars into snakes, and filled the ship with vines and ivy and the sound of flutes. The sailors felt madness coming on them and all dived into the sea, where they were changed into dolphins and made incapable of doing any harm.

Before that time there had been no dolphins. After it, they stood for kindness and virtue in the sea; and the first to learn of their usefulness was the god of the ocean himself, Poseidon – or Neptune, as the Romans called him. When Poseidon was looking for the dark-eyed Amphitrite, to make her his bride, it was a dolphin that found her for him. She had been hiding from him in a cavern of the sea. For this service, Poseidon conferred the highest of all

honours, setting in the sky the constellation of The Dolphin.
If you live in the northern hemisphere you can see it in
July, over in the south-east sky between Aquila and Pega-
sus. And there is another thing that you should see before
we go on. The very word for dolphin, or dolphins, as
written in Greek, is itself a beautiful representation of the
animal's twirling motion through the water:

δελφίς   δελφῖνες

After Poseidon, the first *mortal* who had cause to be
grateful to a dolphin – if mortal he was – was the great
adventurer Odysseus. It is related by the Greek author
Plutarch, in his book *On the Cleverness of Animals*, that when
Odysseus' son Telemachos was a small boy he fell into
deep water, and was saved from drowning by dolphins,
which came to his aid and swam with him to the beach.
'And that was the reason,' says Plutarch, 'why his father
had a dolphin engraved on his ring and emblazoned on
his shield, making his requital to the animal.' If this story
of Plutarch's is true (and admittedly Plutarch lived long
after the age of Odysseus), I think it was the first occasion on which a dolphin showed a kindness to a boy.

Of all the Greek stories of men and dolphins, the one
best known today (because it is mentioned in Shake-
speare) is that of the poet and musician Arion, who was
helped ashore by a dolphin after pirates had cast him
overboard. Arion was not a god but a real person, and
the people of the Greek city of Corinth said that his
adventure took place during the time when Periander was
their king – that is, about six hundred years before Christ.
The story was written down about two hundred years later

THE DIONYSOS CUP by Exekias *c.* 540 B.C.

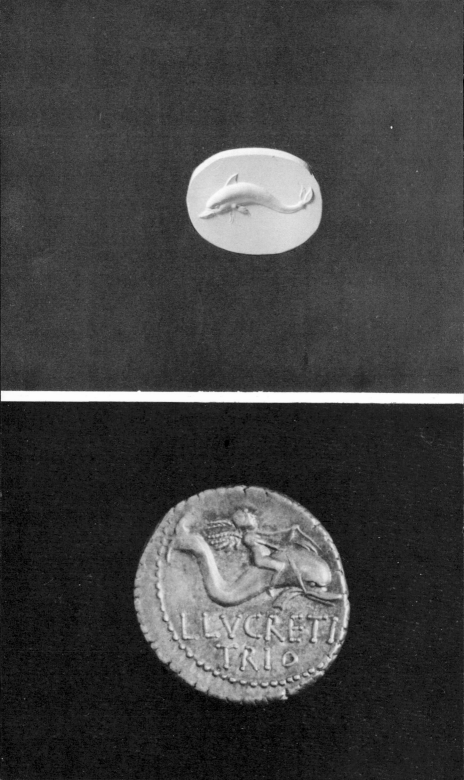

by the historian Herodotos, and there was other evidence as well that something like it really happened.

Arion, who came from the island of Lesbos, sang and played the harp more beautifully than any musician of his time in all the country and islands of Greece. When he sang of heroes, his voice had a manly vigour that everyone admired; when he sang of the feelings of love, the sound that came from the strings of his harp was like a whisper. And he is famous for having perfected a new kind of song for dancing called the dithyramb, which he introduced to his audiences in Corinth. After spending some time at Periander's court, Arion went to the Greek colonies in Italy and Sicily, where I suppose the people had not heard all his songs before. He was victorious at the Sicilian games – at that time the Greeks held contests for poets and musicians along with those for athletes – and he amassed great wealth. With his gifts and prizes in his luggage, he set off again for Corinth. At Taras, which is in the heel of Italy and is now called Taranto, he embarked on a Corinthian vessel, because, says Herodotos, he trusted the Corinthians more than anyone else. But they were another crew of pirates, and when they were out at sea they plotted together to throw Arion overboard and get his money.

Arion, like Dionysos, guessed what was in their minds; on a small ship it is no secret if all the others are planning something together. So he begged them to take his money but spare his life. But they knew that if he got ashore alive he would report them to the king. They told him he must either kill himself, if he wanted to be buried ashore, or jump overboard forthwith.

Seeing there was no chance of their changing their minds, Arion as a last resource begged them to let him end

IMPRESSION from a fifth-century Greek chalcedony gem.

ROMAN COIN, *c.* 74 B.C.

his life with singing. He would put on his singing robes and give them a song, and as soon as he was finished he would go over the stern. He, of all people, must have been familiar with the legend of Orpheus, who with his lyre had charmed wild animals, and softened the hearts of the very guardians of Hell so that he could bring his wife Eurydice back to life. It may be that Arion now hoped to soften the hearts of the Corinthian sailors, or perhaps he merely wished to end his life in a glorious way. At all events, the sailors agreed to his request. Delighted at the prospect of having the world's most famous singer perform for them, they withdrew from the stern and assembled in the middle of the ship. Arion, in his full professional costume, took up his lyre and, standing on the afterdeck, he sang them 'The Orthian', which means 'The Shrill Strain'. It was a high-pitched song addressed to one of the gods.

The ship went on to Corinth. But in the water, according to the story, a dolphin came up to Arion, and it took him on its back to Tainaron, the southernmost point of Greece, now called Cape Matapan. This means, presumably, that the ship must have been blown off its course by a storm. Normally it would not have been going that way – it would have gone straight in through the Gulf of Corinth, a very much shorter route.

From Tainaron, without changing his dress, Arion went by land direct to Corinth, and presented himself at Periander's court. The king at first did not believe his story, but he kept him under guard, and waited for the crew. On their arrival he had them brought before him, and asked if they had anything to tell him about Arion (who was hidden from them in the room). 'Oh yes,' they said, 'we left him safe and sound at Taras.' Arion stepped out, dressed as he was when they last saw him. The astonished sailors could deny the truth no longer. And Arion, let us hope, got all his money and his prizes back.

That is the story as Herodotos heard it from the people of Corinth, and of Arion's own home in Lesbos, two hundred years after it happened. Was it all an absurd invention? I am not sure that it was; but I will leave my reasons till later. Herodotos, at any rate, says that there was in his time an offering of Arion's in the temple at Tainaron, a small bronze figure of a man riding on a dolphin. The figure evidently remained at Tainaron for at least another five hundred years after Herodotos mentioned it, since another Greek historian, Pausanias, saw it there well after the time of Christ, and he says it had an inscription stating that the marvel had occurred during the 29th Olympiad.

It was not long after Arion's lifetime that the city of Taras began to use coins that bore the figure of a man riding on a dolphin. But this figure was not Arion; the coins make it plain that it was Taras, the city's legendary founder, who was a son of the ocean-god Poseidon. He had himself been saved from drowning by a dolphin that was sent to the rescue by his father. In a way this throws doubt on Arion's story of course, for he may simply have heard the Taras legend while he was there, seen an idea in it for a new song (he was presumably always on the lookout for new ones), and spun the tale around his own subsequent escape from the sea. On the other hand, since the coins made their first appearance after Arion's time, *his* adventure may have begun it all. It will be best not to take the facts too literally in Arion's case, but only to remember that there may have been a grain of truth in the story, which later on may not seem so far-fetched.

Arion was grateful to a dolphin for what it had done for him, but in many stories told by the Greeks it was the other way about. One of the oldest tales of a dolphin's gratitude to a man comes from the town of Miletos, on the western coast of the country now called Turkey. At that time it was part of Greece. This tale was first told by Phylarchos, and repeated long afterwards by Athenaios and by Plutarch also.

A man named Koiranos, it was said, saw that some fishermen had caught a dolphin in their net, and were on the point of killing it. He begged them not to, and after paying them money for it he let it go in the sea. Some time later he was shipwrecked off Mykonos, an island to the west, and of all those on board Koiranos alone was rescued – by a dolphin. When he died of old age in his native city, his funeral was held by the seashore, and while the body was being burned a school of dark-backed dolphins appeared in the harbour a short distance away, 'just as if they were joining in the funeral and the mourning for the man'.

From the town of Iasos, in Karia, not far from Miletos, comes another story, and this time it was a boy that the dolphin befriended. There are several Greek stories of friendship between boys and dolphins. This one is told in slightly different versions by two authors of about A.D. 200, Athenaios and Aelian.

Near Iasos there lived a boy named Dionysios. (He was probably named after the wine-god, though his name has the extra 'i' in it.) In the summer, Dionysios and his friends from school were always at the beach, and one day in the water a dolphin came up to him, took him on its back and began to swim out to sea. Dionysios was terrified, but then the dolphin turned back and set him safe on shore again. Afterwards the same dolphin often came to play with him, and crowds gathered. According to Aelian the dolphin regularly appeared 'at the hour when the gymnasium was dismissed'.

This story has an unhappy ending. One day the dolphin in its eagerness followed Dionysios too far in, and it got stranded, and died there on the sand. Presumably it was too heavy and too slippery for Dionysios to get it back to the sea by himself, but was there no one there to help him? Evidently there was not, which suggests that the dolphin's visits had become so commonplace that a crowd no longer gathered when it came.

This marvellous friendship of a boy and a dolphin was reported to Alexander the Great, the young Greek king who had won Karia from the king of Persia. He took it as proof that Poseidon held Dionysios in special favour, and appointed the boy to be High Priest of Poseidon at the temple in Babylon.

These stories became well known all over Greece, and it was natural that people who heard them should feel the desire to reply with similar tales, claiming the same marvels for their own districts. It may be so with the story mentioned by the philosopher Theophrastos, who says that the very same thing as happened at Iasos was also seen at Naupaktos, a town on the gulf of Corinth which is now called Lepanto. And it goes without saying that the people of Taras told a similar tale.

There was even a second story told by the people of Iasos, though it first appeared very much later than the earlier one. In this story, as quoted by Pliny the Elder, the name of the boy was Hermias. Hermias took rides on the dolphin as Dionysios had done, but one time a storm rose quickly, and he was washed off and drowned. I quote the sequel from Plutarch, who tells the story too: 'The dolphin took the body and threw both it and itself together on the land and would not leave until it too had died, thinking it right to share a death for which it imagined it had shared the responsibility. And in memory of this calamity the inhabitants of Iasos have minted their coins with the figure of a boy riding a dolphin.'

This is a good example of the great difference there can be between the things that animals do and the meaning that humans will read into them. The facts as Plutarch heard them might well have been partly true. It is possible that the dolphin did push the boy's body ashore, and possible too that it got stranded itself, and died. But it is a weakness of human beings to look for a human motive in animal actions that may have some other, more natural explanation; and when Plutarch speaks of the dolphin 'thinking it right' to share the boy's death, I think he is doing exactly that.

However, no one need doubt this next story of a dolphin and a boy, which belongs to Plutarch's time but comes from Italy. After several Greek stories, this is the first Roman one. The famous Roman scholar Pliny, who died in the eruption of Vesuvius in A.D. 79, relates it in his *Natural History*, and says it happened during the reign of the Emperor Augustus, which is to say about the time of the boyhood of Jesus, or a little earlier.

The scene was a shallow inlet of the sea not far from where the city of Naples stands today. It was known to the Romans as the Lucrine Lake. Only a narrow strip of land separated it from the sea, and in Roman times, as now, it was full of fish, and famous for its oyster beds. During Augustus' reign, says Pliny, a dolphin that had been brought into the Lucrine Lake developed a marvellous affection for a certain boy in the district of Baiae, a poor man's son, who used to walk round the lake on his way to school at Puteoli.

Now the Romans had a pet name for all dolphins. Because of the shape of their snout they used to call them 'Simo', which is really a Greek word meaning 'Snubnose'. And Pliny says that dolphins would answer to this name, and 'liked it better than any other'.

This boy of Baiae (whose own name has been forgotten) used to stop by the saltwater lake in the middle of the day, and calling 'Simo, Simo', he got the dolphin to come to him, and fed it with pieces of bread. Indeed at any time of day and wherever the dolphin was, even if it was out of sight at the bottom of the lake, it would come when its name was called. And so after a time the boy and the dolphin grew to know each other well, and each lost all fear of the other. And then the boy stepped into the water, and got on to Simo's back.

And the dolphin, says Pliny, would carry him right across the bay to Puteoli to school, and bring him back again in the same way. This went on for several years, until the boy fell ill and died. But the dolphin kept coming to the spot to look for him, 'with a sorrowful air and manifesting every sign of deep affliction, until at last, a thing of which no one felt the slightest doubt, he died purely of sorrow and regret'.

Pliny did not see this dolphin himself, and you may well wonder in that case if the story was true. But he says in the middle of it: 'I should really have felt ashamed to mention this, had not the incident been stated in writing in the works of Maecenas, and Fabianus, and Flavius Alfius and many others.' There are just two doubtful points in the tale: it is unlikely that the dolphin ate bread, though it may have accepted fish; and again, although it may have come to the same place again, and got stranded and died, that would not necessarily be because of 'sorrow and regret'.

The story of the dolphin at Hippo, which I mentioned at the beginning, was known to Pliny too, and he tells it in his *Natural History*. But it happens that his nephew, nowadays known as Pliny the Younger, has told it in far more detail. I have not yet told the whole of the Hippo story, so here it is, as Pliny the Younger told it to his poet friend Caninius, in a letter:

'I have a story for you, which is true, though it has all the qualities of a fable, and is worthy of your lively, elevated, and wholly poetical genius. I heard it the other day at table, when the conversation turned on various miraculous events. The man who told it is completely reliable – though what is that to a poet? However, you could depend on his word even if you were writing history.

'There is in Africa a Roman settlement, near the sea, called Hippo. It is beside a navigable lagoon, and from this lagoon like a sort of river there runs an estuary, whose waters are carried out to sea and back again with the tides. The inhabitants of all ages are very fond of fishing and boating, and of swimming too; especially the boys, who love to idle their time away in play. Their idea of glory is to be carried out to sea, the winner being whoever leaves the shore and his rivals the furthest behind. In a contest of this sort one lad who was bolder than the rest was getting far out, when suddenly a dolphin came up to him. First it swam in front of him, then it followed him, and then went round him. Then it dived under him and took him on its back, and rolled him off again. Then it dived under him again, and to his horror started carrying him out to sea. But then it turned back and restored him to his companions and dry land. The news of this got around, and everyone rushed to see the boy, as if there were something supernatural about him. They eyed him and questioned him, listened to him, and passed his story around.

'Next day they lined the shore, gazing out to sea and watching the lagoon. The boys went swimming, and among them our hero, but with more care this time. The dolphin duly appeared, and made for the boy, who fled with the rest. At that the dolphin, as if inviting him back, started leaping out of the water and diving, and twisting and twirling about. This happened again the next day, and on a third day, and for several days, until the men of Hippo, born and brought up by the sea, began to be ashamed of their fears. They went up to the dolphin, and played with it and called to it. They even touched it, and it encouraged them to stroke it. With experience, they grew venturesome. In particular, the boy who had had the first encounter with it swam beside it in the water, and got on to its back, and was carried to and fro. Feeling that the dolphin knew him and was fond of him, he became fond of the dolphin. There was now no fear on either side, and the boy's confidence and the dolphin's tameness increased together. Other boys, too, swam to the right and left of their friend, urging him on and telling him what to do. What is also remarkable, another dolphin accompanied this one, but only as an onlooker and escort. It did none of the same things, and submitted to none of the same familiarities; it merely conducted the other one to and fro, as the other boys did with their companion.

'Believe it or not (but it is just as true as what I have described) this dolphin that played with boys and gave them rides would also come out on the beach and get dry on the sand, and when it had got warm would return to the sea. It is known that on one of these occasions the Governor's legate, Octavius Avitus, moved by some stupid superstition, poured some precious ointment on the dolphin. To get rid of the strange feeling and the smell, it made for the open sea, and was not seen again for several days, and then it seemed languid and sickly.* However, it soon recovered its strength, and became as playful as before, and was giving rides again. The sight attracted all the officials of the province. But the expense of welcoming and entertaining them during their stay began to exhaust the modest resources of the town; besides, the place itself was beginning to lose its quiet and peaceful character. So it was decided to do away secretly with the cause of the invasion.

'How tenderly, how imaginatively, you will tell this sad tale,' wrote Pliny to his friend. 'What colour you will give

* It was a custom to pour unguent on the statues of the gods, hence Avitus' action was 'superstitious'. But it is just possible that his reasons were better than Pliny thought. Dolphins are very susceptible to overheating; if they are kept out of water and in the sun their skin begins to peel and they grow sick, and it is far more likely that this dolphin's sickness was due to that than to 'the strange feeling and the smell'. Was Avitus, perhaps, trying to soothe the dolphin's sunburn? (It is, of course, unthinkable that the dolphin would have come out on the sand of its own accord. It must have been dragged there.)

it! How you will heighten its effect! Yet there is no need for you to add anything to it. It will suffice merely to make sure that the truth speaks for itself. Farewell.'

I have one more tale from classical times of the love of a dolphin for a boy, and it is another instance of a dolphin's gratitude for kindness done. It is told by the Greek writer Oppian in his long poem called *Halieutica*, or *Fishing*, which was written about a hundred years after Pliny had told the story from Hippo. Like some of the others it comes from the western coast of Asia Minor, or what we now call Turkey. The town of Iasos was on this coast, so was Miletos, and so was the island of this tale, which had the lovely name of Poroselene. It lay near Lesbos (the home of Arion), in the region known to the Greeks as Aeolis. I will give Oppian's version of the story in a moment, but there is one thing not mentioned by Oppian, which we learn from the historian Pausanias.

'I have myself seen the dolphin at Poroselene that re-wards the boy for saving his life,' says Pausanias. 'It had been damaged by fishermen and he cured it. I saw this dolphin obeying his call and carrying him whenever he wanted to ride on it.' That is all Pausanias says; but he has told us of the curing of the wound, which Oppian does not refer to in the following account:

'Nor has all Aeolis forgotten the love of a youth – not long ago but in our own generation – how a dolphin once loved an island boy and in the island it dwelt and ever haunted the haven where ships lay at anchor, even as if it were a townsman and refused to leave its comrade, but abode there and made that its house from the time that it was little till it was a grown cub, like a little child nurtured in the ways of the boy. But when they came to the fullness of vigorous youth, then the boy excelled among the youths and the dolphin in the sea was more excellent in swiftness than all others. Then there was a marvel strange beyond speech or thought for strangers . . . to behold. And report stirred many to hasten to see the wondrous sight, a youth and a dolphin growing up in comradeship, and day by day beside the shore were many gatherings of those who rushed to gaze upon the mighty marvel.

'Then the youth would embark in his boat and row in front of the embayed haven and would call it, shouting the name whereby he had named it even from earliest birth. And the dolphin, like an arrow, when it heard the call of the boy, would speed swiftly and come close to the beloved boat, fawning with its tail and proudly lifting up its head fain to touch the boy. And he would gently caress it with his hands, lovingly greeting his comrade, while it would be eager to come right into the boat beside the boy.

'But when he dived lightly into the brine, it would swim near the youth, its side right by his side and its cheek close by his and touching head with head. Thou wouldst have said that in its love the dolphin was fain to kiss and embrace the youth: in such close companionship it swam. But when he came near the shore, straightway the youth would lay his hand upon its neck and mount on its wet back. And gladly and with understanding it would receive the boy upon its back and would go where the will of the youth drave it, whether over the wide sea afar he commanded it to travel or merely to traverse the space of the haven or to approach the land: it obeyed every behest. No colt for its rider is so tender of mouth and so obedient to the curved bit; no dog trained to the bidding of the hunter is so obedient to follow where he leads; nay, nor any servants are so obedient, when their master bids, to do his will willingly, as that friendly dolphin was obedient to the bidding of the youth, without yokestrap or constraining bridle. And not himself alone would it carry but it would obey any other whom its master bade it and carry him on its back, refusing no labour in its love.

'Such was its friendship for the boy while he lived; but when death took him, first like one sorrowing the dolphin visited the shores in quest of the companion of its youth: you would have said you heard the veritable voice of a mourner – such helpless grief was upon it. And no more, though they called it often, would it hearken to the island townsmen nor would it accept food when offered it, and very soon it vanished from that sea and none marked it any more and it no more visited the place. Doubtless sorrow for the youth that was gone killed it, and with its dead comrade it had been fain to die.'

Ancient delphinology

At the same time as the Greeks and Romans enjoyed telling these stories of individual dolphins and investing them with human virtues, some authors were beginning to write of them in a different way, recording factual observations about the animal's nature, the workings of its body, and its life and habits. As civilised peoples the

Greeks and the Romans were moving away from the half-light of early time when legend filled men's minds. Curiosity, and the reasoning of their philosophers, had led them to the scientific way of thinking, which seeks the explanation of things in the facts themselves rather than in the poetic imagination. One of the first and greatest of the authors who wrote of animals scientifically was Aristotle, who lived four centuries before Christ. In his *History of Animals* he set down a great deal of information about dolphins that was accurate and well observed.

Aristotle had a clear idea of the difference between dolphins and fish. He does not say whether he ever saw one closely or dissected one, but he had found out that dolphins have lungs and a windpipe instead of gills, and that they bear their young alive like quadrupeds and humans, and suckle them with milk; that they have bones 'and not fish-spine', and that although they have no visible ears they can hear sounds in the water. He said that the dolphin makes a squeaking noise when taken from the sea, and he describes their speed in swimming and their high leaps in the air.

He had information about their life-cycle that was mostly correct. 'The young of the dolphin grows rapidly,' he wrote. 'Its period of gestation is ten months. It brings forth its young in summer and never at any other season. . . . Its young accompany it for a considerable period; and, in fact, the creature is remarkable for the strength of its parental affection. It lives for many years; some are known to have lived for more than twenty-five, and some for thirty years; the fact is fishermen nick their tails sometimes and set them adrift again, and by this expedient their ages are ascertained.'

Since he was writing a scientific book, he did not bring fables into it. He merely mentions the *existence* of the tales of dolphins' friendliness to man, without implying that he believed them. But he does tell one story illustrating the devotion of dolphins to each other:

'Among the sea-fishes many stories are told about the dolphin, indicative of his gentle and kindly nature, and of manifestations of passionate attachment to boys, in and about Taras, Karia, and other places. The story goes that, after a dolphin had been caught and wounded off the coast of Karia, a school of dolphins came into the harbour and stopped there until the fisherman let his captive go free; whereupon the school departed.'

He adds another instance of their devotion which has since been treated by some writers as an absurd invention, but is far from being so: 'On one occasion a school of dolphins, large and small, was seen, and two dolphins at a little distance appeared swimming in underneath a little dead dolphin when it was sinking, and supporting it on their backs, trying out of compassion to prevent its being devoured by some predaceous fish.'

Some centuries after Aristotle, and obviously with the *History of Animals* open beside them, both Pliny the Elder and Oppian were writing semi-scientifically of dolphins – Pliny in the manner of someone writing an encyclopaedia and frequently getting things wrong (he was not so careful about his facts as Aristotle), and Oppian in the manner of someone who liked to heighten the truth with poetry. Here is Pliny, in his *Natural History*, copying Aristotle with a few additions of his own:

'They usually roam about in couples, husband and wife. They bear cubs after nine months, in the summer season, occasionally even twins. They suckle their young, as do whales, and even carry them about while weak from infancy; indeed they accompany them for a long time even when grown up, so great is their affection for their offspring. They grow up quickly, and are believed to reach their full size in ten years. They live as much as thirty years, as has been proved by [cutting] the tail of a dolphin for an experiment. They are in retirement for thirty days about the rising of the Dog-Star,* and hide themselves in an unknown manner, which is the more surprising in view of the fact that they cannot breathe under water. They have a habit of sallying out on to the land for an unascertained reason, and they do not die at once after touching earth – in fact they die much more quickly if the [blowhole] is closed up. The dolphin's tongue, unlike the usual structure of aquatic animals, is mobile, and is short and broad, not unlike a pig's tongue. For a voice they have a moan like that of a human being; their back is arched, and their snout turned up, owing to which all of them in a surprising manner answer to the name of "Snubnose", and like it better than any other.'

On the subject of the dolphin's speed, and its prowess in leaping, Pliny follows Aristotle closely, in language of his own. The dolphin, he says, 'is swifter than a bird and darts faster than a javelin'. He makes one slip of the pen: 'They shoot up like arrows from a bow in order to breathe again,' he writes, 'and leap out of the water with such force that they often fly over a ship's sails.' What Aristotle wrote was 'masts', not 'sails'. The two words in Greek are similar.

* It is possible that this is really a reference to the constellation of The Dolphin, which sets when the Dog-Star rises. It is copied from Aristotle.

SILVER COIN from Syracuse, 479 B.C., struck to commemorate
victory over Carthage.

It is from Pliny, not from Aristotle, that we get the first-known description of the dolphin's habit of escorting ships. 'It is not afraid of a human being as something strange to it,' he wrote, 'but comes to meet vessels at sea and sports and gambols round them even when under full sail.' And it is Pliny's honour to have been the first to state expressly that the dolphin is a social animal. 'The dolphins also have a form of public alliance of their own,' is how he puts it in relating Aristotle's story of the behaviour of a school on the coast of Karia. As with Aristotle, I have left out some of Pliny's statements for the present and will return to them later, when they will have more meaning in the light of modern knowledge.

In his poem *Halieutica*, Oppian, like Pliny, mixed fact and fiction. It was not possible for the Romans or the Greeks, relying as they had to on hearsay and information got from fishermen and sailors, to piece together the whole of a dolphin's life-story from birth to death; that, in fact, has become possible only in the twentieth century. Yet just as some of their facts were not quite facts, so some of their fictions were not quite fictions, but coincided with a truth of which they had no actual knowledge. The legend of the origin of dolphins, as I have mentioned already, is itself an example of this.

'Diviner than the dolphins is nothing yet created,' Oppian writes, 'for indeed they were aforetime men, and lived in cities along with mortals; but by the devising of Dionysos they exchanged the land for the sea and put on the form of fishes.'

The truth is that the dolphins did at one time exchange the land for the sea and 'put on the form of fishes'. Dolphins belong to the group of warm-blooded animals called

B.D.—D

TYPICAL COIN from Zankle, showing a dolphin entering a sickle-shaped harbour, *c.* 500 B.C.

SILVER COIN from Taras, *c.* 344 B.C.

cetaceans – meaning the whales, dolphins, and porpoises – which are not fish, but aquatic mammals. And as we know, but the Greeks did not, the remote ancestors of the cetaceans were inhabitants of the land.

Millions of years ago, when the very land itself was different from the land we know today, the beginning of all creatures took place in the sea. The first that evolved could only live in water. These later gave rise to the fishes, and later still there evolved from the fishes some creatures that left the water for the land and developed feet. These first land creatures produced their young as fishes do, by laying eggs that had to be hatched out in the water; and because they needed both land and water (as frogs still do) we call them amphibians. Then came the reptiles, and millions of years later the birds; both reptiles and birds were free of the former dependence on water, because their eggs provided a kind of 'private pond' for their hatching young. About the same time as the birds evolved (that is, within a few million years, one way or the other), there arose from the reptiles a new kind of animal that produced their young alive from their bodies and fed them with milk – like the animals we live among and like ourselves. These were the mammals.

The first mammals lived on the land. But some that had formed the habit of eating fish gradually went back to a life in the sea. Even though they had lungs, as we do, and so could not breathe under water, and even though they had warm blood, and laid no eggs, but produced their young as babies needing their mother's milk, still they established themselves in the sea.

Gradually their whole shape changed, and they began to look like fish. The body that had been developed to suit a life on the land now became streamlined for a life in the sea. The front limbs became a pair of flippers, used for balancing and steering, while the hind limbs disappeared, and the animal used its tail to swim (but the tail was horizontal, and it moved up and down, not sideways like the tail of a fish). On the backs of some a fin appeared, being 'pinched up', as it were, without any bone structure inside it. In these various ways the whales, dolphins, and porpoises are alike, although of course they come in many different sizes and varying shapes, and live and feed in different ways. Some are huge, and some are small; some go about in schools of considerable size, while others go in families or pairs; some live out in the ocean and migrate over long distances, while others are coastal dwellers; and others again live entirely in fresh water, like the dolphins of the Ganges and the Amazon.

The ancestors of all these animals had not exactly 'lived in cities along with mortals', as Oppian said, but they had lived in families by the shore, as the seals and sea-lions do today; and they had helped one another, and grown to be fond, as families are – the mothers fond of the children and the children of their mothers, the females helping one another, and the males in the role of protector to them all.

'But even now,' Oppian continues after mentioning the legend, 'the righteous spirit of men in them preserves human thought and human deeds. For when the twin offspring of their travail come into the light, straightway, soon as they are born they swim and gambol round their mother and enter within her teeth and linger in the maternal mouth; and she for her love suffers them and circles about her children gaily and exulting with exceeding joy. And she gives them her breasts, one to each, that they may suck the sweet milk; for god has given her milk and breasts of like nature to those of women. Thus for a season she nurses them; but, when they attain the strength of youth, straightway their mother leads them in their eagerness to the way of hunting and teaches them the art of catching fish; nor does she part from her children nor forsake them, until they have attained the fullness of their age in limb and strength, but always the parents attend them to keep watch and ward.

'What a marvel shalt thou contemplate in thy heart and what sweet delight, when on a voyage, watching when the wind is fair and the sea is calm, thou shalt see the beautiful herds of dolphins, the desire of the sea; the young go before in a troop like youths unwed, even as if they were going through the changing circle of a mazy dance; behind and not aloof their children come the parents great and splendid, a guardian host, even as in spring the shepherds attend the tender lambs at pasture. ... even so also the parent dolphins attend their children, lest aught untoward encounter them.'

Like Pliny and Aristotle before him, Oppian spoke with wonder of the dolphin's speed:

'The dolphins lord it greatly among the herds of the sea, pluming themselves eminently on their valiance and beauty and their swift speed in the water; for like an arrow they fly through the sea, and fiery and keen is the light which they flash from their eyes, and they descry, I ween, any fish that cowers in a cleft or wraps itself beneath the sands. Even as the eagles are lords among the lightsome birds or lions amid ravenous wild beasts, as serpents are most excellent among reptiles, so are dolphins leaders among fishes. Them as they come no fish dares to approach nor any to look them in the face, but they tremble from afar at the dread leaps and snorting breath of the lord of fishes. When the dolphins set out in quest of food, they huddle before them all the infinite flocks of the sea together driving them in utter rout; they fill with terror every part of the sea, and shady covert and low ravine, and the havens and the bays of the shore are straitened with fishes huddling from every side; and the dolphin devours whichsoever he will, choosing the best of the infinite fishes at hand.'

Like the dolphins themselves, the coastal peoples of those times ate a great deal of fish. With man and dolphin often seeking the same prey, they naturally got to know each other's hunting ways, and the human fishermen learned how to use the dolphins to their own advantage. Obviously, if you could manage to trap a school of fish between your nets and a school of dolphins there was a better chance of a good haul; this suited the dolphins too, and in one place on the south coast of France, near Nîmes, where the mouths of the Rhône flow into the sea, it became a regular practice. We have a vivid account of this from Pliny the Elder, who had probably seen it with his own eyes (unlike some other marvels that he relates) since he was in that province for a time. In A.D. 70 he held the office of tax collector in Gallia Narbonensis.

'In the region of Nîmes in the province of Narbonne,' writes Pliny, 'there is a marsh named Latera where dolphins catch fish in partnership with a human fisherman. At a regular season a countless shoal of mullet rushes out of the narrow mouth of the marsh into the sea, after watching for the turn of the tide, which makes it impossible for nets to be spread across the channel – indeed the nets would be equally incapable of standing the mass of the weight even if the craft of the fish did not watch for the opportunity. For a similar reason they make straight out into the deep water produced by the neighbouring eddies, and hasten to escape from the only place suitable for setting nets. When this is observed by the fishermen – and a crowd collects at the place, as they know the time, and even more because of their keenness for this sport – and when the entire population from the shore shouts as loud as it can, calling for "Snubnose" for the dénouement of the show, the dolphins quickly hear their wishes if a northerly breeze carries the shout out to sea, though if the wind is in the south, against the sound, it carries more slowly; but then too they suddenly hasten to the spot, in order to give their aid. Their line of battle comes into view, and at once deploys in the place where they are to join battle; they bar the passage on the side of the sea and drive the scared mullet into the shallows. Then the fishermen put their nets round them and lift them out of the water with forks. None the less the pace of some mullets leaps over the obstacles: but these are caught by the dolphins, which are satisfied for the time being with merely having killed them, postponing a meal till victory is won. The action is hotly contested, and the dolphins pressing on with the greatest bravery are delighted to be caught in the nets, and for fear that this itself may hasten the enemy's flight, they glide out between the boats and the nets or the swimming fishermen so gradually as not to open ways of escape; none of them try to get away by leaping out of the water, which otherwise they are very fond of doing, unless the nets are put below them. One that gets out thereupon carries on the battle in front of the rampart. When in this way the catch has been completed they tear in pieces the fish that they have killed. But as they are aware that they have had too strenuous a task for only a single day's pay they wait there till the following day, and are given a feed of bread mash dipped in wine, in addition to the fish.' *

Oppian, too, relates that Greek fishermen had the help of dolphins on the shores of the island of Euboea, not far from Athens. This was a different kind of fishing, done at night with the aid of flares. Not having a tidal channel to bring the fish and the dolphins together, the Euboean fishermen used flaming torches in the darkness. The fish were attracted to the lights, and knowing this, the dolphins came up too:

'For when the fishers hasten to the toil of evening fishing, carrying to the fishes the menace of fire, even the swift gleam of the brazen lantern, the dolphins attend them, speeding the slaughter of their common prey. Then the fishes in terror turn away and seek escape, but the dolphins from the outer sea rush together upon them and frighten them and, when they would fain turn to the deep sea, they drive them forth towards the unfriendly land, leaping at them ever and again, even as dogs chasing the wild beast for the hunters and answering bark with bark. And when the fishes flee close to the land, the fishermen easily smite them with the well-pronged trident.

'And there is no way of escape for them, but they dance about in the sea, driven by the fire and by the dolphins, the kings of the sea. But when the work of capture is happily accomplished, then the dolphins draw near and ask the guerdon of their friendship, even their allotted

* It is not at all likely that the dolphins ate the bread mash.

portion of the spoil. And the fishers deny them not, but gladly give them a share of their successful fishing; for if a man sin against them in his arrogance, no more are the dolphins his helpers in fishing.'

Like the earlier examples, these accounts of dolphins assisting human fishermen in ancient times become even more interesting when read in the light of modern knowledge. For it is known now that similar things have been going on, probably for centuries, in widely scattered parts of the world. But I shall come back to this in Part II.

So the dolphin was friendly and gentle – gentle both toward his own kind and toward man – and he was useful, and he may even have saved some lives. No wonder the Greeks should have held him in such high regard.

Did they, in spite of this feeling, kill dolphins for food, as some of their neighbours did? I think it unlikely. There is, of course, the story of Koiranos intervening to prevent a dolphin being cut up; but according to Plutarch's version of that story the fishermen involved were Byzantines, not Greeks. I am inclined to believe that the Greeks behaved toward the dolphin very much as we do toward our friend the horse – who does, of course, get eaten sometimes.

It was a very different story over to the East, and especially around the Black Sea. Xenophon, in describing the March of the Ten Thousand through the country we now call Turkey, says that the Mossynoccians (who lived just south of the Black Sea) had 'slices of dolphin salted away in jars, and in other vessels dolphin blubber, which the Mossynoccians used in the same way as the Greeks use olive oil'.

And the Thracians, inhabitants of a country on the eastern border of Greece, undoubtedly hunted dolphins for their flesh and perhaps their oil. Oppian describes it vividly, and a horrible business it was. For in order to catch them easily the Thracians took cruel advantage of the very thing that dolphins should be honoured for – their mother love.

The Thracian dolphin-hunters went out in light boats that could be rowed easily and turned quickly. When they found a mother dolphin with her young the men would be getting a harpoon ready, but the dolphins would sense no danger. 'Not dreaming that any guile or ill would come upon them from men, [they] fawn upon them as on kindly comrades with delight, rejoicing as they meet their own destruction. Then the fishermen strike swiftly the hurled trident which they call a harpoon, most deadly weapon of the hunt, and smite one of the young dolphins with unthought-of woe. And shrinking back in the bitter anguish of its pain, it straightway dives within the nether brine, racked with torture and grievous agony.'

The brave huntsmen do not waste their own strength in dragging it up by force; they let the line run out and row along behind, until the young dolphin is exhausted with its struggles on the barbed harpoon. Through all this, Oppian says, the mother never leaves her wounded child, but always follows it in its distress. She circles about it as if she were the one that is suffering, and should another of her young be with her she drives it off, to be out of danger. When at length the young one is hauled exhausted to the boat, she too falls into the hunters' hands. 'Unkind and surely greatly sinful,' says Oppian, 'these neither have pity upon her when they see her distress nor bend their heart of iron, but, smiting her also with stroke of brazen harpoon, they slay child and mother together in a common doom.'

If Greek fishermen did anything like this, earlier Greek authors do not mention it. It is true that Aristotle, when he wished to illustrate how sound travels under water, spoke of the hunting of dolphins without disapproval: '. . . though a sound be very slight in the open air, it has a loud and alarming resonance to creatures that hear under water. And this is shown in the capture of the dolphin, for when the hunters have enclosed a shoal of these fishes* with a ring of their canoes, they set up from inside the canoes a loud splashing in the water, and by so doing induce the creatures to run in a shoal high and dry up on the beach, and so capture them while stupefied with the noise.'

But it is not certain that the hunters Aristotle is referring to were Greeks. They could have been Thracians, or any of the neighbouring Mediterranean peoples such as the Greeks used to call 'barbarians'.

Plutarch, in his book *On the Cleverness of Animals*, speaks of dolphins being accidentally caught in nets and being set free again; it is a pleasant bit of nonsense, but in so far as it may be true it gives support to Oppian: 'Now when the dolphin is caught and perceives itself to be trapped in the net, it bides its time, not at all disturbed but well pleased, for it feasts without stint on the fish that have been gathered with no trouble to itself. But as soon as it comes near the shore, it bites its way through the net and makes its escape. Yet if it should not get away in time, on the first occasion it suffers no harm: the fishermen merely

* Aristotle sometimes used this word when speaking of dolphins.

sew rushes to its crest and let it go. But if it is taken a second time, they recognise it from the seam and punish it with a beating. This, however, rarely occurs: most dolphins are grateful for their pardon in the first instance and take care to do no harm in the future.'

Looking over all the known facts, I rather think that Oppian's view of cruelty to dolphins, even though he is alone among Greek writers in expressing it so fervently, may have been fairly widely held. 'The hunting of dolphins,' he declares at one point in his book, 'is immoral, and that man can no more draw nigh to the gods as a welcome sacrificer nor touch their altars with clean hands, but pollutes those who share the same roof with him, who willingly devises destruction for the dolphins. For equally with human slaughter the gods abhor the deathly doom of the monarchs of the deep.'

Already at that date the new teaching of the Christians was spreading through the Mediterranean countries, and in the early Christian Church the dolphin was held up as a symbol. He stood for Swiftness, Diligence, and Love. But I think the Christian teachers may have learned rather than taught this truth, when they came among the Greeks.

ᴏ   ᴏ   ᴏ   ᴏ

DOLPHINS IN MODERN BIOLOGY

BOOK III. (*Duodecimo*), CHAPTER I
(*Huzza Porpoise*). – *This is the common porpoise found almost all over the globe. The name is
of my own bestowal; for there are more than
one sort of porpoises, and something must be
done to distinguish them.*

HERMAN MELVILLE: *Moby Dick*
CHAPTER XXXII

THERE ARE MANY DIFFERENT DOLPHINS
in the various oceans of the world, but two of them are
better known to man than any of the others, either because of their habits or because they are more numerous.
Both are found in the Mediterranean Sea, so when the
Greeks or the Romans speak of a dolphin it is likely to be
one of their number that is meant, and the dolphin at
Hippo, for instance, may have been what we now call a
Common Dolphin (in scientific language *Delphinus delphis*)
or it could have been one of the slightly larger species
known as the Bottlenosed Dolphin (*Tursiops truncatus*).
Both are fond of coastal waters, but the Common Dolphin
is also found well out to sea; or, as Oppian said, 'The
dolphins rejoice both in the echoing shores and dwell in
the deep seas, and there is no sea without dolphins, for
Poseidon loves them exceedingly.' The Greeks of course
did not have different names for these two species. To
them, any dolphin was simply a δελφίς, as to the Romans
it was a *delphinus*, and they were not familiar with all the
other species known to us today. The Common Dolphins
are the ones that play round ships at sea in the friendly
way that has commended them to sailors over many centuries. They will join a ship and stay alongside, sometimes
for hours at a time, gliding and playing in the bow wave
with obvious enjoyment and sometimes even getting a
ride in it, cunningly exploiting the laws of hydrodynamics

and travelling with no visible movement of their bodies. They go about in families or schools, and groups of them will come up for air together, in a rolling movement so perfectly timed that you feel there must be some hidden communication between them. The Bottlenosed Dolphins occasionally follow ships too, though not in quite the same playful way. It is the Common Dolphins that are met in great numbers in tropical waters, sometimes in schools so large that the sea is literally frothing with them as they sport and leap in the waves.

It seems likely that the Common Dolphin is the more numerous species of the two throughout the world, though no one can be sure. In some places – the western shores of the Atlantic, for example – the Bottlenosed Dolphin is by far the more frequently seen. For so graceful a creature, 'Bottlenose' seems an ugly name, but it is hardly more unkind than the Romans' name of 'Snubnose'. It was probably given in the first place by sailors. There used to be a type of gin bottle which the snout of a *Tursiops* was said to resemble.

In America dolphins of any kind are usually called porpoises, and the same thing tends to happen in New Zealand. To me the name that comes from the Greek seems both more beautiful and more correct, and I prefer to use it, reserving 'porpoise' as the English do for those slightly smaller members of the dolphin family that have no beak (their mouth being merely an opening in a blunt-shaped head) and whose teeth are spade-shaped instead of conical. This is the distinction generally made in countries remembering what they owe to the Greeks. The word porpoise, by the way, comes from the French *porc-poisson*, meaning 'fish-pig', so it is even more uncomplimentary than 'Bottlenose'. I personally cannot find it in me to be as fond of the porpoise as I am of the dolphin, and I incline to a feeling that Pliny seems to have had: 'The creatures called porpoises* have a resemblance to dolphins (at the same time they are distinguished from them by a certain gloomy air, as they lack the sportive nature of the dolphin), but in their snouts they have a close resemblance to the maleficence of dogfish.'

Apart from all these differences, real and imagined, dolphins and porpoises are virtually the same animal, for they both belong to the family of cetaceans known to zoologists as the Delphinidae, and all the Delphinidae in turn are Odontoceti, or toothed cetaceans. Since these terms can be confusing when encountered for the first time and will be turning up again, I had better explain them here.

Beginning at the top, we have first of all the Cetacea, or all the whales, dolphins, and porpoises, constituting one of the Orders of the animal kingdom (a distinction actually first made by Aristotle). And the living Cetacea in turn are divided into two Suborders: the Mystacoceti (literally, 'moustache whales') which have inside their mouths a huge moustache-like sieve, of a substance called baleen,† for straining plankton out of the sea; and the Odontoceti, which are equipped with teeth for catching fish, or larger prey of a solid nature. Most of the toothed cetaceans are very much smaller than the baleen whales, which are generally giants. The only very large odontocete is the Sperm Whale, which feeds on a giant prey. With its narrow, underslung jaw, the Sperm Whale catches and kills

---

* The Latin word here is *thursiones*, whence comes our *Tursiops*.

† More commonly, but somewhat misleadingly, known as whalebone.

B.D.—E

the Giant Squid of the ocean depths, as well as various fishes. The most famous of all cetaceans, Moby Dick, was a white Sperm Whale, apparently one of the albino freaks that are known to occur from time to time.

The Odontoceti in their turn are divided into several families and subfamilies that vary a good deal in size and habits, but this book is concerned almost solely with one family, the Delphinidae, and for the present with only two of its species, the two really well-known species already mentioned. Later on we shall encounter some of the other Delphinidae – the so-called Killer Whales, for instance, and their meeker cousins, the pilot whales, and one very famous Risso's Dolphin; and also the interesting fresh-water dolphins of the Ganges and Amazon and other rivers, which belong to another family. But so much more is known of our friends from the Mediterranean and the Atlantic – and especially of *Tursiops* – that these two must inevitably dominate this book, and to some extent steal the show.

Common Dolphins, fully grown, are about eight feet long, and they can be distinguished at sea by their beautiful markings. Like most other dolphins, they have a 'cloak' of darker colour on their backs and a belly of lighter colour, but there is a sharp classical purity about the markings of a typical *Delphinus* which alone would have made them attractive to the Greeks. Their cloak has a clear-cut edge, their eyes are handsomely ringed in black against the white, and halfway along the body there is a sort of saddle, where the cloak dips downward to a point – their best distinguishing feature in the ocean. Between the forehead and the beak an incised black groove runs round their face – (like a V when viewed from above) –

from one eye to the other. Some of the dolphins on Greek coins are clearly Common Dolphins, since they show this groove, though possibly the Greeks were also familiar with a rarer kind, now called *Prodelphinus euphrosyne*, whose markings are as beautiful as its name. Euphrosyne, or Joyfulness, was one of the three Graces in Greek poetry.

It is evidently the Common Dolphin that Herman Melville so delightfully describes in *Moby Dick*, under the name of the Huzza Porpoise: 'I call him thus, because he always swims in hilarious shoals, which upon the broad sea keep tossing themselves to heaven like caps in a Fourth-of-July crowd. Their appearance is generally hailed with delight by the mariner. Full of fine spirits, they invariably come from the breezy billows to windward. They are the lads that always live before the wind. They are accounted a lucky omen. If you yourself can withstand three cheers at beholding these vivacious fish, then heaven help ye; the spirit of godly gamesomeness is not in ye. A well-fed, plump Huzza Porpoise will yield you one good gallon of good oil. But the fine and delicate fluid extracted from his jaws is exceedingly valuable. It is in request among jewellers and watchmakers. Sailors put it on their hones. Porpoise meat is good eating, you know. It may never have occurred to you that a porpoise spouts. Indeed, his spout is so small that it is not very readily discernible. But the next time you have a chance, watch him; and you will then see the great sperm-whale himself in miniature.'

There is another beautiful description of *Delphinus* in Patrick Leigh Fermor's *Mani: Travels in the Southern Peloponnese*. 'These creatures bring a blessing with them. No day in which they have played a part is like other days. I first saw them at dusk, many years ago, on the way to

Mount Athos. A whole troop appeared alongside the steamer, racing her and keeping us company for three-quarters of an hour. Slowly it grew darker and as night fell the phosphorescent water turned them into fishes of pale fire. White-hot flames whirled from them. When they leapt from the water they shook off a million fiery diamonds, and when they plunged, it was a fall of comets spinning down fathom after fathom – league upon league of dark sky, it seemed – in whirling incandescent vortices, always to rise again; till at last, streaming down all together as though the heavens were falling and each trailing a ribbon of blazing and feathery wake they became a far-away constellation on the sea's floor. They suddenly turned and vanished, dying away along the abyss like ghosts.'

Fermor was told by the captain of a Greek steamer that sailors in those waters today call out to *delphinia* by the name Vasili. They have 'a special way of shouting', the captain said, and when the dolphins hear it they stop dead with their heads out, looking round to see who has called. When the caller repeats the name, 'they join him, like lightning'. He also relates the experience of a Greek friend who was in a small boat listening to music on a portable radio. A number of dolphins came so close that they rocked the boat, and when the radio was put away to prevent its getting wet they departed.

Bottlenosed Dolphins are both longer and plumper than the Common Dolphin, and their markings are not so 'classical', being altogether softer. Their upper parts and tails are black, or rather a sort of purplish grey, fading to white on the underside. There is no suggestion of a 'saddle' on their flanks, and their eye lies in the dark part of the face, with no special markings of its own. They have another feature that is absent from the face of the Common Dolphin – the line of the mouth when it is closed has a gentle, upward curve that gives them a most amiable expression, very near to being a smile. As you can see from the photographs, *Tursiops* often wears a look of smug contentment more expressive than anything seen in a cat or a dog.

To distinguish the Common and Bottlenosed Dolphins at sea, consider first the size: *Tursiops* ten or eleven feet long and roly-poly, but *Delphinus* only eight, and slender. Then the markings: *Delphinus* clean and classical, with the 'saddle' behind his dorsal fin, and the black-ringed eye; but *Tursiops* more softly shaded, without the saddle, and without the ring around the eye. And then, if you are near enough, the face and mouth: *Delphinus* has the groove but *Tursiops* has the upturned mouth, or 'smile'. Of course there are various other dolphins that you might encounter, and other books to help identify them. Let us turn now to what a dolphin is, disregarding the things that distinguish one genus or species from another.

∘   ∘   ∘   ∘

A dolphin – or a porpoise, or a whale, or any of the Cetacea – is an animal that lives entirely in the sea. I say 'animal' here deliberately, using the word as many people still unconsciously use it, meaning really a mammal and not a fish or reptile. It is by being 'animals' in this popular sense that the cetaceans are unusual in the sea. They are *mammals*, whose prehistoric, dry-land ancestors had legs and hair, warm blood, and lungs like our own, and bore their young alive and suckled them with milk.

Except for two of the original four limbs, dolphins still

have all of these things (even a few whiskers, to begin with!) and they bear and suckle their young like quadrupeds – but in the sea. In terms of evolution they have not been back there so very long: perhaps sixty million years or so. Yet so thoroughly have they assumed the fish-like form that they now look more like fish than many fishes do, and if they get stranded on the shore they die.

How did they make this transformation? I shall try to explain it in a simple way; but first a warning is necessary. I shall be talking about the outward changes – about the *course* of evolution, not about the process itself. And in all our thinking about how animals evolved it is important to avoid what is called a teleological approach. That is, you must not think of the changes and adaptations as having a 'purpose', foreseen and worked toward as if from a desire to adapt. It is true that if we could watch the long procession of generations passing before our eyes they might give every *appearance* of pursuing such a purpose, but this would be an illusion – an illusion not unlike what happens when we view a motion film and are in darkness half the time. The generations are the 'stills', as it were, contained in the separate frames of the film, and none of them is actually moving (in the sense of trying to advance its adaptation to the environment) any more than one of the figures in a cinema frame is moving; yet when the frames are flicked over, movement of their images appears to occur.

What actually happens in the evolutionary process is that all those creatures not possessing advantages which would help them to survive drop out (you may think of them, if you like, as the missing shots between the frames), and those possessing them accumulate them, and so build up the illusion of purposeful change. In other words, it is not the individual animal that changes, it is the species. This may sound like splitting hairs, but it is important to remember that, while it may be true to say the dolphins 'became adapted', it would not be true to say they 'adapted themselves'.

The warning given, we can turn to the changes that occurred, and the most satisfactory way of doing this is to forget the motion film now and think instead of a model, which can display the course of events without being too specific.

Take a lump of plasticine about twice as big as your thumb, and make a rough four-legged animal, not too much like any that you know. Make the legs fairly short and provide a substantial tail, like that of an otter.* You could make the head something like a pig's and, if you are neat with your fingers, give it two small ears and prick in a pair of nostrils. Forget about hair; the ancestor we are thinking of may have lost most of its hair already, like pigs or hippopotami. As a further refinement you could include a faint suggestion of a hump on the back – not quite as big as that of a zebu or a camel; perhaps more like a bison's. *No horns*.

Now imagine that this animal for some reason is going to start seeking its food (and maybe refuge from some enemy or competitor) in the water, starting possibly in swamps and rivers or possibly by the sea. Begin a sort of smoothing-out process, working backward from the head, as if your fingers were imitating the flow of water over the

---

* That is, a pointed tail with a thick, strong base which is useful in swimming, but not flattened like a beaver's tail.

animal's body, remembering always that this is not what happened in nature but only the appearance of what happened. You won't be able to do everything at once, but pretend that your fingers are those of the Creator himself. Take your time. Take millions of years!

Starting at the front, push in the head so that the neck fills up, and wipe the ears away, leaving only pinholes. Flatten the front legs into flippers, and take the hind legs off entirely. *Keep them near you.* Now attend to the tail region. First, pinch it from the sides so that it is narrow like the hinder part of a fish (or caudal peduncle, to give it the scientific name). Then pinch the *end* of it in the other direction to give the beginnings of horizontal tail flukes. This is where you will need the discarded plasticine; adding the extra bits, form a dolphin's tail, with its gracefully curved edges and a notch at the centre. Shape the dorsal fin as well, and do it with style.

Now go back to the nose. Shape it into a dolphin's beak and, with fingers as dexterous as those of the Creator, simultaneously cause the nostril holes to move to the top of the head, uniting them there in a single crescent-shaped blowhole. (This migration of the blowhole began at the beginning, of course, like everything else.) Add finishing touches, such as shaping the flippers to their proper form, and perhaps supplying the smile of a *Tursiops*.

As an elaboration of all this you could, if you wish, give your creature a halfway stage, making it resemble a seal for a while, with hind legs bent back toward a tail not yet formed for propulsion. This might be misleading, however, because the seals of today are not necessarily the dolphins of some future time. Now put the model away (an old-fashioned receipt spike makes a suitable stand, if you want to keep him without spoiling his flippers), and we shall return to the dolphins of nature.

It is the skeleton rather than the soft parts of an animal which records the evolutionary history of a species, and the skeletons of whales and dolphins tell us much about their past. The bones of a cetacean neck, for instance, bear witness to the process of compression: the seven neck vertebrae that most mammals have are there but are compressed in length, and in some species even fused together. Most whales and dolphins cannot bend their necks; but *Tursiops*, as we shall see, is able to.

The hind limbs are gone, although not without leaving any trace. If you were to dissect the body of a stranded dolphin you would find, embedded in the muscles in the region where you would expect them, two bones that represent the vanished hips. They are not connected to the backbone, and are slowly being 'dissolved away'. When the skeleton of a whale or dolphin is exhibited in a museum, these vestigial hip bones have to be hung in position on separate wires.

The bones of the flippers (which, by the way, are purely balancing and steering fins, and are not used as oars) are connected to the rest of the skeleton just as our own arms are, and they include the various bones of an 'arm' and of a 'hand'; the five sets of 'fingers' are there, enclosed in one mitten of flesh. In the embryo of an unborn dolphin, these fingers can be seen quite clearly, giving the flipper a somewhat scalloped appearance.

There are no bones at all inside the dorsal fin or the tail flukes. These consist purely of fibrous tissue, being pinched out, as I have said, for their separate purposes – the fin for balancing, the tail for propulsion. People who have touched a dolphin's dorsal fin say that it feels like smooth wet rubber; and children who have ridden on a dolphin's back have sat against it, using it like the cantle of a saddle.

The skull is prolonged into a beak, not only in the dolphins, where you can see it, but in the porpoises as well, and the teeth are different from those of most land mammals. There are more of them, eighty to ninety in *Tursiops*, and they are all the same size and shape. This is because the dolphin's mouth is only used for catching food, and not for chewing it. He catches a fish and, after turning it crosswise and crushing it, swallows it whole, head first. He therefore has no incisors, canines, or molars; his teeth are all conical, sharp, and curved slightly backwards – excellent for holding a slippery prey. A porpoise's teeth, however, are different, with a sort of spade-shaped head, but still uniform.

When a dolphin opens its mouth while swimming, water does not necessarily get into the lungs. It is a mistake to think of the mouth as something it breathes through, for the air passage from the blowhole on top of the head passes down to the windpipe without opening into the mouth, as with us. However (and some earlier accounts have now to be corrected on this point), the trachea evidently can be retracted.* Dolphins in captivity have been seen indulging in something very like a belch under water (that is, emitting air from the mouth), and in an attempt at artificial respiration an air tube has been inserted in the respiratory passage by way of the mouth.

Of a dolphin's ear, all that can be seen from the outside is a tiny pinhole in the side of the head – so small that Aris-

---

* For this information I am indebted to Forrest G. Wood, Jr, of whom more will be heard in subsequent pages.

totle missed it completely. Any outer ear that the cetaceans' ancestors may have had has long since been streamlined away and the hole closed up against the water pressure. But (as Aristotle knew) the dolphin has excellent hearing under water. Waterborne sounds are conducted with great efficiency along the closed-up tube to a hearing mechanism equalled only by that of the bats. This I shall describe in detail later on, when we come to the *use* that the dolphin makes of its auditory sense.

A dolphin's eye is as lively to look at as the eye of a horse. It can be moved about, it closes with an eyelid, and does not have that glassy look of a fish's eye but is visibly the eye of a mammal. It is also shiny at night, like a cat's. The dolphin is not shortsighted out of water. Captive dolphins have shown that they can see the movements of a hand waved fifty feet away, and if a fish is thrown to them from the same distance they can follow its path through the air and invariably catch it, if it is thrown at all accurately. Moreover, when a wild dolphin is captured, it will follow a person's movements warily, with this eye that seems not to belong to the sea.

The colouring of the skin, dark above and light below, exhibits the principle of countershading seen in many other mammals and in some fishes. This makes it a little more difficult for the dolphins' enemies to see them. From above, they merge with the darkness beneath, and from below, their pale underbelly shows indistinctly against the light. This shading may represent nothing more than the effect of sunlight on their skin, but it is a good example of an adaptation exhibiting apparent purpose, though none may have been 'intended'. It would appear to be a useful protective feature; yet not all dolphins have it. The Pilot

Whales, for instance, or Blackfish, are black all over,* and some of the vividly marked black-and-white dolphins of the colder waters are far from being countershaded. So much for the structure and the outward appearance of the dolphin's body. Now for how it all works.

⟡   ⟡   ⟡   ⟡

How does a dolphin swim? I have already said that it does not use its flippers to pull itself along. It drives itself forward with its tail. So does a fish, but there are striking differences between the two. To begin with, a dolphin's tail is horizontal, not vertical; this is no accident, but is full of meaning. Everyone knows that fishes, like reptiles, bend their backbones *sideways* when they swim. They can flick away to left or right on sensing danger or to chase their prey, but they cannot dart upward or downward nearly so efficiently. A dolphin, on the other hand, bends its backbone vertically, like a galloping dog, and its tail moves up and down. It is therefore well equipped for diving suddenly or for leaping to the surface. But, for an interesting reason, it can *also* turn sideways as quickly as a frightened fish, even when swimming at speed.

The reason is this: in order to give the best possible up-and-down pull to the tail flukes, the muscles in a dolphin's caudal peduncle have been built out, so to speak, above and below the spinal column. This makes it streamlined for the vertical movement (the caudal peduncle is very much thinner than the side view suggests) and at the same time produces flattened sides, which make possible the rapid turn. This is different from the fishes.

* They are, however, strictly nocturnal feeders, and so have less need of countershading.

In most fishes – the salmon for example – the caudal peduncle when moving presents its *widest* surface to the water. In other words the 'lever' in a fish is part and parcel with the tail, and is itself employed in pushing against the water. (In fact if a fish's caudal fin is cut off, the fish can still swim quite well, whereas a dolphin without its tail flukes would be in difficulty.) Yet in certain fishes, such as tuna, mackerel, and herring, the caudal peduncle is narrowed but it is not at the same time built out sideways for leverage.

Which makes the more efficient use of energy? The dolphin's long and streamlined lever, like the shaft of a racing oar, or the salmon's somewhat more primitive arrangement, in which the lever itself does some of the sculling? It would take an extremely clever biologist to prove one system 'better' than the other – and it might be a waste of time.

For the dolphin, the ability to come *upward* quickly and easily is obviously of supreme importance. If he were not equipped to do so he would not exist today, and that is the main advantage of his type of tail; but it does seem a great additional advantage that he can dart up and down or sideways equally well, without having to turn on his side and so impair his vision and orientation. Most interesting of all, in my view, is the fact that in the dolphin's tail we see a mammalian characteristic, developed originally for its suitability on land, turning out to be a significant advantage in the sea.

How *fast* can a dolphin swim? Is Aristotle's statement true, that the dolphin is 'the fleetest of all animals, marine and terrestrial'? If land animals are brought into the picture, it is not true. A dolphin's best speed, deduced from the speed of ships that have been accompanied and passed, is thought to be somewhere between 25 and 30 miles an hour, and this is far behind the swiftest quadrupeds. The cheetah, for example, can touch a speed of 70 miles an hour, the lion has been measured at 50, and even a running elephant does 25! In the sea, conditions are entirely different, since resistance by the water is so much greater than resistance by the air, and also a different method of propulsion is involved; so the only comparison of any value is with the fishes, and even among them it would seem that the dolphin has its challengers, at any rate for short bursts. The tuna has been said to be capable of a burst of 35 m.p.h. or more, and it is thought that the billfish also may be faster than the dolphin. However, there is a lot of guesswork in these estimates; fish speeds when measured scientifically are usually found to be much lower than they appeared to subjective observation, and the tuna may not be capable of anything like 35 m.p.h. Nor has anyone yet measured the speed of the dolphin scientifically in the ocean. The best we can say is that dolphins have been seen easily accompanying and cutting in front of ships doing 20 knots (or 22·5 m.p.h.). Yet even this, surely, is not necessarily their top speed. What dolphins can do when *accompanying* ships for pleasure – when deliberately staying beside them and playing at the surface, and darting ahead for fun – is hardly a reliable measure of what they might do when below the surface and afraid; for they certainly can swim fast more easily when well submerged. At the surface, the turbulence of the water round their bodies is a drag. Below it, they gain full advantage from their streamlined shape and from their tail strokes, and they also escape wave motion.

All the same, there has been some puzzlement as to how a dolphin *can* do 25 miles an hour, for the fact of the matter is that for an aquatic animal of the dolphin's size and muscular capacity this is a very high speed indeed. Tests with rigid models of a dolphin have shown that the amount of energy theoretically necessary to drive the body through sea water at 25 m.p.h. is about ten times the amount its muscles can produce – unless in some marvellous fashion the dolphin's muscles have been given a far greater output than those of an athlete or a dog. Since physiologists have been agreed for some time that this is not likely, the only alternative is that the dolphin must possess some way of reducing the friction drag, and the secret of this is something that designers of submarines and torpedoes, and also of high-speed aircraft, would very much like to know.

The problem was first discussed in 1936 by Professor Sir James Gray of Cambridge University, after whom it became known as Gray's Paradox, and it is also mentioned in his book *How Animals Move*. Gray suggested that the movements of the rear part of the dolphin's body probably played some part in reducing the turbulence there, as did the fact that the water near the tail was actually being moved backward relative to the surrounding water – both being advantages not enjoyed by a rigid model. But he still had to conclude that, if the dolphin did not have more powerful muscles than other mammals, then in some way not yet understood, 'Nature's design for a dolphin is much more efficient than any submarine or torpedo yet produced by man.'

As might be expected, the problem was soon the subject of research, and not of a disinterested sort. And the answer, which would be astonishing were it not high time we ceased to be astonished by anything about the dolphin, has since been found and published.

The story behind this discovery is interesting in itself. In 1938 Max O. Kramer, of the German Research Institute for Aeronautics in Berlin, was granted German Patent No. 669897, entitled Device for the Reduction of Friction Drag. The patent suggested a means by which 'oscillations in the wall-near flow' could be reduced where fluids were passing over rigid surfaces; it employed an arrangement of narrowly spaced wires mounted close to the surface and parallel to the flow. The war interrupted Kramer's test work on this device. He worked on German guided missiles instead.

After the war he went to the United States to work on research for the Navy. While crossing the Atlantic he saw dolphins for the first time, and was fascinated by their performance. He studied the subject and soon was convinced that the dolphin 'has solved the problem of laminar flow' – that is, of controlling turbulence at the skin and reducing the friction drag. In California in 1955 he obtained some dolphin skin and examined it under the microscope. He found that the pigmented outer skin, far from being a waterproof covering, was actually a waterlogged, soft coating to a fatty, harder inner skin. It is one sixteenth of an inch thick and is itself composed of an outer diaphragm covering a multitude of narrow vertical ducts filled with spongy material which is soaked with water. This skin (that is, the surface diaphragm and the mass of little ducts) dries out and becomes brittle when allowed to, and its weight then is only one fifth of its weight when wet. Kramer realised that it was 'probably a highly refined

THIS PHOTOGRAPH of *Tursiops* shows well many features described in the text, particularly the movement of the head.

realisation of the basic idea expressed in my 1938 patent'. Its pressure-sensitive outer diaphragm, being supported on a multitude of tiny pillars with the waterlogged spongy material between them, would be able to take up all the minute oscillations that are caused at any one point of the surface when waviness or turbulence of the wall-near flow passes by.

Kramer simulated the dolphin's coating in rubber, making a sort of sandwich of rubber sheeting separated by multitudes of tiny rubber stubs, and using fluids of differing viscosity as the filling. He put this coating on slender rigid models, and tested the drag in flows up to 40 miles an hour. He described the results – with a backing of technical detail which I am omitting here – in an article in the *New Scientist* for May 1960. When used on a model four feet long, the coating reduced the drag coefficient by as much as 60 per cent. 'After the tests,' Dr Kramer claims, 'the dolphins' secret ceased to exist. Their astonishing performance had found its technical explanation.'

It remains for research and development to perfect the coatings, and Kramer's own company is working on this in California. They may well be used, he says, 'in certain aircraft, hydroplanes, and possibly even pipelines'. It is very much to be hoped that this secret, extracted by a guided-missiles expert from the most peaceable of mammals, will be applied to purposes of peace.

There is another phenomenon connected with the dolphin's skin which may have a bearing on its speed performance. Frank Essapian (some of whose photographs illustrate this book) has found with the help of high-speed photography that when dolphins are accelerating and swimming at high speed they develop certain large-scale

B.D.—F

A school of dolphins surfacing to breathe.

Dolphins playing with a turtle.

wrinkles on their sides. These are not parallel to the flow, but usually at right angles to it (though sometimes they slope away toward the tail). It seems possible that they also may have their part to play – perhaps in conjunction with the microscopic wrinkles employed in Kramer's coating – in the dolphin's attaining of laminar flow.

These arrangements are concerned only with *maximum* speed; and, maximum speed aside, it appears that the dolphin possesses a quite different form of superiority over the fishes, inasmuch as it can swim at high speed for very much longer periods than they are able to. The reasons for this are tied up with other factors, so I shall have to come back to them; but before I leave the subject of the dolphin's swimming there is one other remarkable aspect of it to be mentioned.

Dolphins have been seen, as I said, riding just in front of ships' bows with no visible motion of their bodies, and evidently getting a free ride from the bow wave. They were seen doing this in the Gulf of Panama in 1948 by Alfred H. Woodcock of the Woods Hole Oceanographic Institution, who observed them carefully and timed them with a stopwatch, and wrote a contribution to *Nature* about it. The animals did it both in their normal swimming position and on their sides (when it was easier to be certain that there was no movement of the tail). One dolphin travelled on its side in this manner for nearly a minute, covering 300 metres at the vessel's speed of 10 knots. Other dolphins out of reach of the bow wave were swimming vigorously in the normal way.

Over the years since this was published a controversy has been going on in scientific journals as to how the dolphin performs the trick, for it appeared to flout the laws of hydrodynamics even when the help of laminar flow was allowed for. Four explanations have been offered, using three different assumptions about the position of the dolphin in relation to the ship's bow wave.

First there was the joint 'preliminary attempt' of A. H. Woodcock and A. F. McBride (1951), who worked on the assumption that the bow-riding dolphin is planing on the bow wave with the help of gravity – that is, 'falling' down its continually advancing slope (like a soaring bird or man-made glider in an updraught), and overcoming the drag by laminar flow. However, the weight of a dolphin lying in sea water is fairly small (9 pounds or so for a 200-pound animal with its lungs collapsed, giving only 3 pounds of forward thrust at a slope of 20 degrees), so that this explanation is difficult to sustain, even when laminar flow is assumed. Then in 1953 W. D. Hayes of the United States Office of Naval Research pointed out that near the wave surface buoyancy is not a vertical force but is tilted forward (because the isobars are not horizontal but are parallel to the wave slope). This would help, and the lightness of the submerged dolphin would not matter; its total weight, not its submerged weight, would be the significant factor – so long as it was lying near the wave surface.

The third explanation came in 1959 when P. F. Scholander of the Scripps Institution of Oceanography entered the controversy with a different view about the position of the dolphin's body. He declared that wave-riding dolphins he had seen were not lying actually in the wave slope but forward of it, and by placing their *tail flukes* in the upwelling part of the wave at a certain angle were converting that energy to a forward thrust. He had tested this theory experimentally from the bows of a research vessel at sea, placing a tiltable, streamlined vane in the top of the vessel's bow wave and measuring the forward thrust it got at various angles. He considered it possible. But his equipment was crude and his method open to objections, and Hayes was able to show that a dolphin that tried to do what Scholander described would not be able to maintain equilibrium; it would be tipping over all the time. Admitting defeat in the argument to Hayes, in December 1959, Scholander nevertheless very properly maintained that 'these rascals are a graveyard to our wits'. 'Again we must bow to the dolphin,' he said.

And there the matter rested for a year until Andrew A. Fejer and Richard H. Backus of the Woods Hole Oceanographic Institution came up with a fourth and quite different explanation,* which does not depend on where the dolphin is in relation to the *visible* wave that a ship's bow makes.

The visible and vertical wave that wells up beside a ship's bow is actually the side issue of something larger and more important, which for purposes of hydrodynamic calculations can best be considered in the horizontal plane. As a ship drives forward in the water it creates a pressure field just in front of the stem which is not visible to us but which a dolphin could detect by its sense of touch. It exists not only near the surface (where the bow wave represents a vertical escapement from it) but extends as far down as the stem does. If a dolphin were to get its body into this horizontal pressure field (and Fejer and Backus have seen bow-riders at depths of six feet or so, and arranged in layers), it would be pushed along much as we are blown forward on a street in a high wind.

* In *Nature*, November 26, 1960, pages 700–703.

Fejer and Backus observed dolphins riding apparently in this manner in front of small vessels that do not generate conspicuous bow waves. They would approach from a distance in a purposeful way, turn parallel to the ship when ahead of it, and then be gently overtaken, to assume bow-riding stations from one to five feet ahead of the stem. There they might stay for only a few seconds, or for 'as long as an hour or more'. Often eight or ten animals would join the ship together and spend ten or fifteen minutes there, till they dropped away in ones and twos.

Their flukes would be anything from several inches to five feet ahead of the stem, and the lateral spread might be three feet to either side of it; occasionally the flukes might be a foot or so behind the stem. As to depth: the animals might be two to six feet below the surface and might 'be arranged in two or even three layers'. Of course they rose to breathe from time to time. They were seen lying on their sides and upside down, and even 'slowly revolving about their long axis'.

One special position was noted by Fejer and Backus, which was a little more common in *Tursiops* than in *Delphinus* (both of which were bow riders at different times). A dolphin on its side was occasionally seen to bend its tail firmly downward. It is possible that dolphins lying in a normal position were doing this too (though in this case it would be hard to tell from above), but when it was done side-on the dolphin almost always had its back to the ship – that is, its flukes were laid against the invisible pressure field.

Fejer and Backus take care to make plain the complexity of the forces, posture, and movements involved in bow riding. In reality, they say, the dolphins are 'now coasting, now swimming to make adjustments in their position relative to the ship or to change their posture, now coasting again', and 'the resulting picture is quite involved'. But their explanation is the most fully reasoned of the four that have been offered, and is probably in the end the right one; and it does not exclude the possibility that dolphins sometimes also exploit the other means of getting propulsion from the visible, upwelling bow wave. No doubt some underwater photography of the sort that is possible from the underwater chamber on the stem of Captain Cousteau's research vessel will some day settle the matter. So much, meanwhile, for the dolphin's locomotion.

When you see a pair of dolphins from the shore, you usually see their backs coming over in a slow smooth roll as if they were fixed on an invisible wheel, turning under the sea. This is their normal breathing roll. If you were near enough, you would be able to hear the sound they make: there is a sudden puff and gasp as each dolphin appears; he empties his lungs and refills them, and then the valve of his blowhole snaps shut again: *pff-HOO-p*. It all takes less than a second.

When necessary, they can stay below the surface for several minutes without coming up for air, and whales of course can stay down much longer. This fact is of great interest to man, so a good deal of experiment (using dolphins, not whales!) has been devoted to finding out how it is done.

It is not by having larger lungs. A dolphin's lungs are relatively no bigger than our own (and a whale's are only half as big), so the answer must lie somewhere else. It appears that there are four distinct and parallel techniques, and possibly a fifth, by which dolphins make better use of their breathing.

The first is that every time they take a breath, dolphins renew far more of the air in their lungs than we do; the second is that they extract more of the oxygen from it; the third, that they are able to hold more oxygen in the tissue of their muscles; the fourth, that when they dive their heart beats more slowly; and the possible fifth (which I think is still conjecture) is that they have a sort of priority system for supplying the brain with unused blood, and so delaying the stimulus to take the next breath.

When we take an ordinary breath, we renew only about a quarter of the air in our lungs, and we extract from the new air only a small part of the oxygen it contains. When a respirometer was strapped over the blowhole of a dolphin it was found that with each breath he took the animal changed three-quarters of the air in his lungs, and was extracting oxygen at twice our rate. In other words, each normal breath was worth six times as much to the dolphin as ours is to us.

The breath once taken, better use is then made of it. The muscles of a whale or a dolphin contain more myoglobin than those of a land mammal (which is what makes whale or dolphin meat so dark in colour), and this enables the animal to store up more oxygen in its muscles than we can. Moreover, electrocardiograms obtained from Bottlenosed Dolphins diving in semi-liberty have shown that the heartbeat is slowed down by about 50 per cent on diving.

The 'priority device', it is thought, exploits a peculiarity of the way in which the brain is caused to give the signal for the taking of another breath. Strange as this may seem, it is not a lack of oxygen which makes us gasp for air when we feel we are suffocating, but an excess of carbon dioxide in the blood being fed to the brain. (People can quietly die in a room full of hydrogen with no sensation of suffocating; and when oxygen is used in artificial respiration, carbon dioxide is mixed with it to stimulate the patient to breathe again. This is one reason why the mouth-to-mouth method works well.) In mammals there is a network of arteries massed around the spinal cord and parts of the brain, known as the *rete mirabile*. Since these arteries are much developed in the Cetacea it is thought that they may serve as a reservoir of unused blood for the brain, whereby the muscles can simply go ahead and incur an oxygen debt, and the stimulus to breathe again is withheld for a while.

Or, to put cetacean breathing in financial terms: dolphins operate on a high turnover to begin with; they extract more profits; they have better banking facilities; they can cut their overheads when pressed; and if, in spite of all this, their bank account gets into the red, they can arrange it with the accountant not to tell the manager just yet.

On the other hand, a dolphin's normal breathing is very nearly the best he can do. It is equivalent to what we do when we are running, and he can increase it only slightly in an emergency; we can increase our rate much more than he can when we have to. To decide which system is 'better' seems to raise imponderable questions of economic philosophy: the dolphin would appear to be a believer in *inflation*. And with that we perhaps ought to leave the subject of cetacean breathing. Let us do so by way of the blowhole.

People who have handled stranded dolphins have been

surprised to find, when they put a hand over the blow-hole, that the animal's breath is warm and steamy. Although its skin may be cold to the touch, its whole body inside is warm like ours. Thus we say, readily enough, that a mammal is warm-blooded, whereas fishes and reptiles are not. But is the meaning of the term always understood? The point is not merely that a mammal's body is *warm*, but that it has a thermostat for keeping the temperature *even*. When we speak of fishes and reptiles as being cold-blooded, what is really meant is that their body temperature, instead of being held at one level, goes up and down with the environment: tropical or Arctic fishes are as warm or as cold as the water they are in; lizards in the shade are cool, lizards in the sun are hot. Our system, though it raises difficulties for animals that live in a very cold or changeable environment, is in general the more efficient and the more adaptable. And in the case of the dolphin this is the source of a distinct advantage, once again, over its neighbours and competitors the fishes.

I mentioned the dolphin's ability to swim at high speed for longer periods than fishes, and said I would return to the reasons. In his book *How Animals Move*, Sir James Gray says: 'The dolphin certainly does not tire anything like so quickly as a fish. Dolphins are mammals; they are warm-blooded, and they breathe with lungs as we do. These advantages enable the animal to renew its muscular energy much faster than a cold-blooded fish can.' He did not elaborate this statement in his own book, but he has been kind enough to do so by letter for this one:

'I think there can be little doubt that the ability of a dolphin to maintain high swimming speeds is associated with the fact that it is a mammal and as such possesses a double circulation of blood through the heart. The oxygenated blood leaves the left ventricle under considerable pressure and consequently the amount of oxygenated blood reaching the muscles in unit time is very much greater than in the case of a fish where the blood is oxygenated in the gills; the pressure of blood in the dorsal aorta of a fish is *very* much lower than that of a mammal. In both cases the muscles fatigue unless supplied with oxygen and in the long run the output of power from the muscles is determined by the rate at which they can be supplied with oxygen. It may well be that the chemical changes which are necessary for overcoming fatigue go on quicker at a higher temperature although I do not know of any experimental proof. In short, the dolphin *is* better off than a fish because it has a mammalian type of circulation, and it may also be better off because it works at a higher temperature – but this may be of secondary importance.'

It is, of course, necessary for all warm-blooded animals to prevent too much loss occurring of the heat they obtain from their food, and the land mammals, especially, need to be able to adjust themselves to changes of temperature between night and day, and between the seasons. Most of them therefore have a jacket of hair or fur.

But hair would be useless as a heat-retaining jacket to an animal that lives entirely in the water, and the dolphins have long since parted with all they had; all, that is, except a few whiskers on the snout of the newborn infant, which disappear about a fortnight after birth.

Instead of hair, the cetaceans now have an insulating layer of fat, or blubber; and once again we find a mammalian characteristic assisting the dolphins' adaptation to the sea. The layer of blubber has contributed to the perfecting of their streamlined shape, and to making them buoyant (so that they do not need to keep their lungs full in order to float), and it may be that it goes further than that. It is possibly thanks to the blubber that their skin is enabled to go into the wrinkles that Frank Essapian has photographed on the flanks of an accelerating dolphin. These wrinkles presumably play some part in the overcoming of friction.

It is because of the enormous quantities of blubber around their bodies, of course, that whales are hunted and killed. Dolphins, thank goodness, are so much smaller that they are not worth the trouble of catching nowadays. That they were taken on the shores of the Black Sea in the time of the Greeks and pickled we know from Xenophon. Long before that, Nordic tribes took porpoises from the North Sea for food, as the bones in their middens have revealed, and the people of Minoan Crete had harpoons that were probably used for catching dolphins. 'Porpesse pudding' was an English dish of Tudor times, and in Catholic countries porpoise meat has in the past been decreed to be fish so that it could be eaten on Fridays; the precolonial American Indians hunted dolphins in the Bay of Fundy, and for a while during this century there was a dolphin fishery at Cape Hatteras (the oil from their jaws was in demand for watches and other fine mechanisms); dolphins or porpoises are still hunted for food in Scandinavian waters and Japan, the Russians slaughter them by the thousand in the Black Sea, and I have a friend who has eaten dolphin sandwiches in Venice. But, generally speaking, dolphins escape the barbed harpoons of predatory man today for the simple reason that they are small, and their blubber is only about one inch thick.

Which raises the question: is it *because* their blubber is thin that dolphins live mainly in the warmer waters, or is it the other way about? The answer is, really neither. It is more a question of size. The largest cetaceans, the whales, are able to frequent the coldest waters because they have sufficient bulk in relation to skin area to retain the heat their food provides without losing too much of it through the skin. But a dolphin, for every pound of his weight, has a much greater area of skin, and therefore of possible heat loss, than a whale. Or put it this way: a large joint of beef will stay hot on the table much longer than a plate of chops, and a whale can keep warm more easily than a dolphin. One southern member of the smaller dolphins, *Lagenorhynchus wilsoni*, has been seen just north of the Antarctic pack ice during the summer months, but by and large the only members of the Delphinidae commonly found near the icecaps are the very big ones known as Killer Whales.

All these facts lead to an interesting conclusion about the cetaceans: the fact of their being mammals did not disqualify them for a successful life in the sea but, rather, it did the opposite. One might expect to find that all those adaptive devices specifically evolved for a life on the land would automatically be hindrances in the sea, but that is far from being the case. The vertical flexion of the back-bone and the powerful tail (with the incidental result of the caudal peduncle being useful also for a sideways turn), warm blood, superior muscle power and the capacity for long bursts of exertion, the use of the blubber layer for streamlining and buoyancy, the particular structure of the skin that appears to facilitate control of laminar flow – all these are *mammalian* characteristics, and all are positive advantages to the dolphin. In short, it is always a good thing to be a mammal, even in the sea.

There is another striking paradox about the cetaceans which seems worth mentioning here. It was stated some sixty years ago, when the available information was primitive compared with what is available now, by F. E. Beddard in his *A Book of Whales*, and it has to do with the remarkable degree to which the cetaceans have approximated the fishlike form. Beddard had been trying to classify the various cetaceans with reference to each other, and had found difficulty because the various members of the Order were all so *similar*. In this they resembled the birds. The reason, he perceived, was that to inhabit the water was a mode of life 'entirely foreign to their organisation'. In the case of the fishes, the 'whole organisation was fitted to the marine environment' and so there was ample room for much variation without affecting the necessary essentials: 'What could be more utterly different in shape,' Beddard asked, 'than a skate and an eel,* or a sunfish and a sole?' But with the whales and dolphins it was precisely the other way about.

As with the birds, so with the cetaceans. 'So little divergence from the suitable structure would be just the fatal straw . . . a slight structural divergence might easily prove fatal to the perfect fulfilment of their functions.' So the dolphins are, in quite a real sense, 'more fishlike than the fishes'.

* Zoologists will notice that Beddard has weakened his case by an unfortunate choice of examples at this point; skate and eel are not equally 'fishes' but are as wide apart zoologically as a turtle and a mammal. There is some truth in the argument, all the same.

Family life

◌ ◌ ◌ ◌

'They usually roam about in couples, husband and wife; they bear cubs after nine months, in the summer season, occasionally even twins. They suckle their young, as do whales, and even carry them about while weak from infancy; indeed they accompany them for a long time even when grown up, so great is their affection for their offspring.' This is a touching account of Pliny's, and essentially a true one, of something of which far more is understood today. As millions of Americans know, the establishment of marine aquariums has made it possible to observe a dolphin's birth and growth under far better conditions than were ever enjoyed by Greek or Roman sailors. We also know far more about the *background* of a dolphin birth – about the evolution of mammalian reproduction, and the how and the why of it.

Here I must briefly retrace the story of the cetaceans' double change from sea to land and back again. I have shown what this means in terms of the dolphin's *structure*, but what it means in terms of reproduction is a separate story.

When life first moved out of the sea to the land, all the animals had to adapt their method of reproduction by one means or another. The amphibians dodged the problem by going back to the water at breeding time – as frogs do when they lay the eggs that hatch out tadpoles. The reptiles, and the birds too, got round it by laying an egg with a hard shell, containing, as I have said, its own 'private pond', and enough food in the form of yolk for the young one to develop before being hatched out. The mammals solved it by keeping the young inside the mother's body until it was ready to be born – but not to look after itself – and then feeding the infant with milk and protecting and teaching it during its first months of life. This makes the infant mammal completely dependent on its mother, but, once again, in the long run it produces a more successful animal. For by remaining with its mother throughout the dependent phase the infant mammal learns a great deal from her about its environment and its food supplies and possible enemies, and it *goes on learning*. And in the case of the higher animals it 'learns to learn', or becomes intelligent, and so carries the habit beyond the dependent phase. This, combined with their physical adaptability, goes far to explain why the mammals have got along so much better on the earth than any reptiles or amphibians. Equally it helps to explain the success of the cetaceans in the sea.

But some mammals are more dependent on their mothers in the first months of their life than others, and as a rule the most dependent and helpless infants are those of the 'higher' species. Or put it another way: the longer time the infant spends with its mother, the more it learns and the more it becomes capable of learning. The babies of humans, monkeys, dogs, and cats are all like this: kittens, for example, are born blind, and human babies don't see very well at first; and none of these animals can walk to begin with. Yet the infants of grazing animals such as deer, horses, and cattle, whose mothers must go on grazing after the birth, are born with good sight and the ability to walk, and even run, alongside their mothers. There is some evidence that the immediate ancestors of the cetaceans were animals of this kind, for it has been found that the chemistry of their blood relates them to the cud-chewing animals. They also have three stomachs (of which the first resembles a rumen) and a long intestine, which is characteristic of herbivores.

And so now, many millions of years after their double change from sea to land and back again, dolphins are born like calves and foals and lambs – dependent on their mothers but able to move around freely from the beginning.

The newborn dolphin is shaped exactly like its parent, it is nearly a third of her length, and its eyes are wide open. It can swim to the surface for a breath within seconds of being born, and from that moment it swims beside its mother, easily keeping up with her if the parent senses danger.

Obviously, then, a baby dolphin is born far more 'complete' than a kitten or a puppy, and to make this possible the mother must keep it inside her body for a longer period. In this again she resembles the cud-chewing mammals of the land. Also, she can only afford to have one infant at a time. A cat, which is able to conceal its kittens and keep them together in some protected place, can bring them forth, blind and helpless, after keeping them in her body for a mere two months. But a mother dolphin must make her infant ready for the ocean, and she takes twelve months to do so (not ten, as Aristotle said). As for dolphins having anything like a litter, it is plain that in both the bearing and the tending of them, that would be difficult for the mother.*

* But there is record of two foetuses being found in a pregnant *Delphinus*, and unborn twins and triplets have come to light on whaling ships.

10   Courting dolphins rubbing past each oth

Once it is born, there are special arrangements for the baby dolphin to grow up quickly. The mother's milk (which, incidentally, has a fishy smell and an oily taste) is extremely rich. Compared with human milk, it contains six times as much protein, the special growing food, and far more fat. A human baby fed on its mother's milk doubles its own weight in the first six months, but a baby dolphin increases its weight two or three times as fast.

It has also been contrived that the newborn dolphin shall get its milk without difficulty under water. As any human parent knows, a baby cannot suck without breathing as well. The infant dolphin obviously cannot do that, so there is a device whereby the mother can give it a large gulp of milk in one go. From the glands that make her milk, this is run off into little reservoirs, and as soon as she feels the infant squeezing her teat with its tongue she can squirt out some of the contents of the appropriate reservoir by contracting the surrounding muscles – a scheme that I find commands great admiration among human mothers. The baby can swallow the milk, and go to the surface for a breath if it wants to, before coming back for the milk from the other teat. Sometimes the mother rolls on her side to help the newborn baby to suckle, but after a week or two she lets it do the rolling over. If a mother should lose her infant and be uncomfortable with the milk, she can squirt it out unaided. Correlated with these arrangements, cetaceans do not have the flexible lips that other mammals have for suckling.

Naturally, these things have not all been learned by watching dolphins in the sea. It is true that the Greeks and Romans knew a good many of them, or guessed that they

B.D.—G

YOUNG DOLPHIN suckling.

THE BIRTH of a dolphin.

must be so; and every so often some mariner with the gift of observation is able to record a fleeting glimpse of dolphin life in the wild. My compatriot Adrian Hayter, for one, who sailed alone from England to New Zealand a few years ago, has vividly described in his book *Sheila in the Wind* what he saw one morning in the western Mediterranean when his yacht *Sheila* was off the North African coast:

'Next morning a school of porpoises joined *Sheila*, and were either playing some game which allowed the greatest intimacy and demanded the highest standards of aquatic skill, or else were very much in love. They circled the bow in pairs about six feet under water; one nuzzled the other, which, after playful and unmistakably feminine protest, turned over on its back to show the startlingly white belly. The other moved over her and together they swam in graceful curves as one united being. Still together they rose upwards, and only just before breaking surface the female turned upright, and flank to flank in perfect harmony they emerged, blew, and dived as one. As they entered the water the female again turned gracefully over as she curved away, and the male covered her again. The grace and perfect harmony was beautiful to watch.'

Such glimpses are rare, however, and for the complete knowledge that we now possess of the cetacean life cycle the world is indebted to those who established the Marine Studios aquarium at Marineland in Florida. Here, since 1938 (with a four-year gap during the war) Bottlenosed Dolphins have been successfully kept captive, in good health and contentment, in a replica of the normal aquatic environment, with fishes small and large, and rays, eels, and turtles, and sometimes even sharks for company. From the railings round the circular tank, and through the portholes in the sides beneath, millions of Americans have now seen them – millions without including televiewers – and over the years the staff and visiting research scientists have watched everything the dolphins do, learning the facts about many things that Aristotle and Pliny were only able to assume. Among them is the marvel of the dolphin's birth,* and the courtship and mating that occur in the previous year.

As everyone who has read *The Sea Around Us* knows, there is a springtime even in the ocean, and it is in the spring that dolphins begin their courtship. The male – I shall call him Simo – sometimes begins to pay attention to one of the females by a sort of posturing in front of her. He swims into position and forms his body into an S-curve, his head uplifted and his tail bent down. He holds this for a few seconds, and then goes back to his normal swimming. Later, Simo may swim up under the female – I shall call her Delphine – and pause with his head just beneath her tail; she responds by patting his head with her tail flukes in a gently affectionate way that is quite distinct from her swimming movements. Or Simo will swim over Delphine's back, lightly stroking her with his flippers as he passes; sometimes he will turn over on his back and do this from underneath, stroking her two flippers with his. These actions, which may go on for half an hour or more, are the gentler portion of the dolphins' courtship, and they usually take place when the animals are resting.

* The first recorded cetacean birth in captivity occurred at Brighton Aquarium, England, in 1914, when a Common Porpoise delivered a stillborn calf. The first *live* birth in captivity occurred at Marine Studios on February 26, 1947, when the Bottlenosed Dolphin Mona – who was pregnant when captured off the Florida coast – delivered a healthy female infant, Spray.

More vigorous things occur when the dolphins are feeling energetic. There is sometimes a series of repeated rushes by the male, who makes for a head-on collision with Delphine but at the last moment turns aside sufficiently to produce a vigorous rubbing of their bodies. This activity usually goes on for a few minutes only, and may be accompanied by a certain amount of enthusiastic noise. Occasionally at such times Delphine will play the coquette and rush away from Simo, perhaps leaping right out of the water as if to escape him. When this happens he will dart for the spot where she is likely to enter the water again, to be vigorously rubbed once more. The result may be a sort of dolphin ballet, and a beautiful sight it must be, judging by Plate 10. When their energies have died down, Simo and Delphine will resume swimming quietly together.

There are times when either Simo or Delphine will nuzzle the other with the snout closed, or will make gentle biting movements with the open jaws, perhaps grasping a flipper and allowing it to be drawn away without leaving tooth marks. Should another male get in the way at any of these times, or seem to be taking an unwanted interest, Simo may show his displeasure by clapping his jaws together with a loud noise that can be heard outside the tank from fifteen feet away.

In due course, as Aristotle wrote twenty-three centuries ago, 'It is the same with the dolphin and with all cetaceans; that is to say, they come side by side, male and female, and mate, and the act extends over a time which is neither very short nor very long.'

The mother *Tursiops*, as I have said, takes almost exactly a year in the gestation of her infant, and during the latter half of it she begins to behave differently from the other females in the tank. She lives a little apart from them, spending more time on her own than dolphins usually do, or else she spends her time in the company of one particular female, a chosen friend who later assists at the birth. (Something very similar to this occurs among the elephants too, as J. H. Williams has related in his *Elephant Bill*.) In one case at Marine Studios, two females that were pregnant simultaneously spent most of their time together; in another case, a young female who from her earliest days had shown a preference for the company of her own mother sought her as the chosen companion.

As the time for the birth draws nearer and her abdomen grows larger with the developing infant, the pregnant dolphin begins to do what seem like prenatal exercises. She will be seen to bend her tail downward, and sometimes her head as well, forming her body into an arch with all the muscles taut and holding it like that for a few seconds. Then she curves back in the other direction, straining upward with her head and tail. One of the mother dolphins at Marine Studios at times did this continuously for an hour or more in the weeks just before her infant was born.

Pregnant dolphins at Marine Studios have also been most appreciative of the stiff brushes anchored to the floor of the tank for the animals to scratch themselves upon. They have been seen getting the bristles into the opening through which the infant is to be born, wriggling back and forth to remove an itch. Another habit of late pregnancy is a kind of yawning, or stretching of the mouth and tongue, and sometimes a female who is soon to give birth stays at the surface breathing for two or three minutes at a time. And thus the day itself arrives.

To humans, birth is always a marvellous thing because it stirs our imaginations to think of the new life beginning; and it must be difficult when a dolphin birth is taking place at Marineland not to be lost in wonder at the beauty of it. It all takes place, of course, in that magical blue light existing just below the surface of water in which the dolphins themselves, until they come near, appear as blue-grey shadowy ghosts, not quite substantial. On the bottom there are white ripples of sunlight from the surface, and the dolphins' bodies catch these up like veils as they slide through the silent water.

The birth begins, but not as the births of land mammals commonly begin. Dolphins emerge tail first, which is rather unusual. When this was first observed at Marine Studios, it was thought the reason must be to prevent the baby from being drowned by its trying to breathe under water – because a normal dolphin birth may take anything up to two hours altogether, and is seldom completed in less than half an hour. But it is not absolutely certain that that *is* the reason.* The tail emerges, folded and soft, and for a while it is all that can be seen. The mother continues alternately swimming and straining her muscles, and in time the trunk appears, and then the flippers, and finally the whole falls free. And in what follows, the mother dolphin lives up to her reputation of early Christian times, when she was a symbol of Swiftness, Diligence, and Love.

In the instant following the birth the mother whirls round, sharply and swiftly. This puts her in a position to

* Out of many births that have now been observed at Marine Studios, only one was head first, and the infant in that case did not drown. It was a quick birth, however, and things might have gone differently had the baby not fallen free within a few minutes of getting its head into the water.

help the infant rise to the surface for its first breath, and it may also serve to break the umbilical cord before the infant rises. Normally the young one, with its eyes wide open already, will wriggle its own way to the surface, beating its tail at double speed and getting there in a few seconds; but in case of difficulty the mother is at hand to help.

This final moment of the birth has its effect on *all* the dolphins in the tank, and not only the females. Sensing the climax, they assemble around and beneath the mother, drawn by their instinct to attend an occasion that does indeed concern them all – for in an animal that brings forth only a single infant at a time, the infant's survival is essential for the sake of the species.

Next, another remarkable thing is seen: the mother, far from having to care for her infant alone, finds that she has the support and the very practical assistance of the other females. As she follows her infant to the surface for its first breath, the appointed 'auntie' will probably swim beside her, and the others, whether young or old and whether or not they are experienced in motherhood themselves, stand ready to help protect the infant. For instance, they will keep away any sharks, or any male dolphins that may make a nuisance of themselves. When the mother whirls and the cord breaks there is a small cloud of blood in the water for a moment, and this naturally attracts the sharks if any are present. The attendant females surround the mother and keep them away. The male dolphins sometimes show unwelcome curiosity toward the infant, and they have been known to get quite nasty, even trying to nip it with their teeth, though never savagely. The females then will fend them off, and they continue helping the mother in this way for several weeks.

There is a notable difference here between dolphins and those rather different animals the seals. In a seal colony the infants are often injured, squashed, and sat on because of quarrels between the adults, and numbers of them die in their rocky nurseries. The sea, it would seem, confers a benediction on those who entrust themselves entirely to her care.

In all this, though, there is nothing to match the loving care that the dolphin mother herself displays. Her first concern is to see that the infant gets up to breathe. If it does not swim to the surface itself as soon as the cord is broken, she will nudge it upward with her snout. On one occasion when a dolphin was born dead at Marineland the mother did every possible thing that might have helped, even trying to lift its body from the bottom by taking a flipper in her mouth. On another occasion an infant died during the night, and in the morning the mother was found supporting its body at the surface. How long she had been doing so, no one knew. There, surely, were Diligence and Love. The mother of a dead infant has also been seen trying to lift it by grasping its body between her flippers, as some remote ancestor of hers may once have used its 'hands'.

The newborn dolphin is normally about three feet long – nearly a third of its mother's length – and weighs about twenty-five pounds. Its head, like a human baby's, is big for its body, and on its snout are the bristles mentioned earlier. Along its sides at first are vertical creases of unpigmented skin, due to the sideways-curved position in the womb. These are on both sides, so the foetus apparently changes its flexion and position from time to time. The fins and tail flukes, folded when inside the womb, are soft and flexible at first, and the dorsal fin flops to the side it was folded on. It stiffens up within a few days. There are teeth under the baby's gums, but they do not cut through until a few weeks later.

Within twenty-four hours of its birth the baby begins to nose round under its mother to find her teats. There are two of them, set in grooves toward her tail. When they are found, the baby dolphin receives its first squirt of milk, and may leave a little cloud of it in the water on letting go the teat. After that it comes back for more at intervals of twenty minutes or so.

Life has now begun for another young dolphin. But for several weeks it will continue to be under the watchful eye of its mother, who, as Oppian knew, will 'not forsake him, but always attend him, to keep watch and ward'. Notwithstanding it is such an advanced infant compared with some other newborn mammals, it is still a toddler. Its swimming is rather wobbly at first, and to keep up with its mother it has to beat its tail much faster than she does, so that it looks like any human child trotting beside the parent. Its inexperience is also shown in the way it surfaces to breathe. During the first two months or so the young dolphin shoots its head right out of the water, only to fall back with a splash. It takes practice to develop the characteristic smooth roll of the adult dolphin.

During this stage the mother does not like her infant to stray more than about ten feet from her. If it does, she quickly noses it back. Generally it takes up station beside her dorsal fin, in much the same way as a foal trots beside its mother in the paddock, and with its outside eye shut tight! This seems to be a protected position adopted instinctively. Very often the 'auntie' or another female will swim alongside as well, so that the infant is guarded between *two* dorsal fins.

This swimming beside the mother's fin suggests an interesting possibility: there may be some connection between it and the willingness of female dolphins, at any rate, to accept the presence of a human child in a similar position. A female dolphin might feel there is something right about a child's holding on to her dorsal fin and being towed in the place where she is used to having her infant swim. (When dolphins and children make friends, this towing by the fin is usually the first sort of riding that occurs; proper riding, with the child astride the dolphin's back, only comes later.)

If this is so, does it mean that all the friendly dolphins in the Greek and Roman stories were females? The younger Pliny's description of what happened at Hippo contains one fact that might have some bearing on the point. There was a second dolphin, he says in his letter, that swam with the friendly one, but only as an onlooker and escort: It neither played the same tricks nor submitted to the same familiarities, it merely accompanied the other to and fro, just as the other boys did with their companion.

What made the difference between the two? Was the playful one a female – or was it merely a *young* dolphin, with the mother watching its play from near at hand? Too late to find out now, but here is a suggestion for future observers of friendly dolphins: any female dolphin that becomes friendly enough to roll on her back for a scratch will reveal the presence of her teats. They lie in grooves on either side of the vent, toward the tail, where the udder would be in a cow (and during the nursing period they bulge out noticeably). Perhaps in future people who encounter friendly dolphins in the sea will try to determine their sex, and by the time we ourselves are as ancient as the ancient Greeks and Romans the world may know whether it is the females that give the rides.

Dolphins, like any other animals, need to sleep. In captivity they do so by lying a foot or two below the surface, with the tail dangling slightly and the eyes closed. A few strokes of the tail are enough to bring them up for a breath every half minute or so, and usually their eyes will open once or twice in the intervals between. This sounds unrestful, but it is hardly different from our own ability, when asleep, to pull up the bedclothes without waking. A sleeping infant dolphin dozes just beneath its mother's tail, and both rise to breathe together.

At Marineland the dolphins do not take a long sleep as we do throughout the night, but get what they need in short catnaps (like cows, to which they are thought to be ancestrally related). Usually all the members of a family sleep together, though perhaps this only applies in captivity. A 'family', here, means one male and one or two females, with any young ones that are still attached to their mothers. At Marineland it has been found that keeping to this pattern in the tank makes for happiness among the dolphins. If more than one adult male is kept in the exhibit there is likely to be trouble; on the other hand if there is no man in the house, the women tend to quarrel! When there *is* any trouble, the dolphins seldom bite one another, at any rate not savagely. Most of their fighting is confined to hitting with snout and tail – though even this can cause the death of a young one.

The family unit is one thing, a school of dolphins is

another. I have not yet described their schooling, and in some ways it is even more important to them than their family life. Dolphins are gregarious animals; they live in a herd, and at times of danger they act as a herd, usually with the biggest male as leader. At Marineland, if something happens that disturbs the dolphins, such as the arrival of a newly captured shark, or any unfamiliar object, they will all bunch together and begin swimming in tight formation, with the youngest and their mothers in the middle. At such moments any little differences between them are forgotten. The bull forgets his annoyance of a few moments before with the cheeky youngsters, the females forget their jealousies, and all become united, the bull determining what they do. Usually they all swim round for a time, craning their necks toward whatever it is that has frightened them, keeping together and alert. In the open sea no doubt the school either combines to attack an enemy or makes off, according to what the leader does. But the school itself is also its own defence, simply by being together in one place. In the early days at Marineland the dolphins once had occasion to combine against sharks, and by butting them in the sides and gills caused them to die. They had good reason for this enmity: in the stomach of one Tiger Shark that died soon after its capture in the sea the curator found most of the skeleton of a Bottlenosed Dolphin.

A week or two after its birth the infant begins to venture away from its place of safety beside its mother's fin, and one of the first things it does is to nuzzle round her head, rubbing itself against her face and snout. This is another behaviour pattern with a striking resemblance to an adult habit: the fondness of dolphins for playing round the bows of ships might well be, in part, a recalling of this early pleasure.*

When three months or so have passed, the mother begins to relax her guard, but as long as the infant is still being suckled she does not drop it completely. How important her care can be became apparent in 1954, when one of the Marineland dolphins, Spray, had an infant which for some reason she neglected. Usually a mother will not let her newborn infant wander more than a few feet away, and even when feeding time comes round she will go to the feeding platform, snatch a fish for herself, and hurry back to the young one. But Spray frequently allowed her infant to wander, and at feeding times she would abandon it to join in the scramble for fish. The infant died after fifteen days. Its stomach was found to be quite empty, and it also had a broken jaw, presumably from a bump that a good mother would have prevented.

Suckling normally goes on for about a year and a half, but a young dolphin begins to take occasional solid food at the age of six months or so. When the time comes for the infant to have his first piece of squid or mullet from the feeding basket, he probably only plays with it at first (and maybe loses it to one of the others). When at length he tries the food, he sometimes gets indigestion.

When fully grown, the dolphins eat about eighteen to twenty pounds of fish each per day. They do not treat the rest of the aquarium exhibit as their food supply – though newly introduced specimens go in some risk of their lives, and from time to time an unlucky fish of longer acquaintance will become a plaything and be eaten after being

* See also page 193.

toyed with in cat-and-mouse fashion. The regular food supply is caught in the open sea and frozen, and dispensed at public feeding times as in any other zoo. Ordinarily the dolphins are content with that. In the wild they eat a variety of small fishes, according to where they live, such as mullet and herring and butterfish. The Danish biologist Eschricht has recorded that in the stomach of one *Delphinus delphis* he counted the ear stones of 7596 little fishes that had recently been consumed. How Oppian would have delighted in the knowledge of that fact!

How long does a dolphin live? It would be interesting to know, but this is one piece of knowledge they may continue to deny us, except in captivity. The life span of the large mammals varies a good deal. Baleen whales are believed to reach the age of 50. Chimpanzees live to 40 or thereabouts, and Chacma Baboons to 45; lions live to 30, but tigers only to 19, giraffes to 28, and hippopotami to 41. The mammal with the longest life span next to man is the elephant, which has been known to reach 69. More comparable with the dolphin are seals and sea lions, which live about 20 years. A Polar Bear has lived to 34. These figures* are of course all for animals in captivity, except the whale. Because of the interruption of the war, Marine Studios has been in continuous operation only since 1946, and it will be some years yet before sufficient animals have lived out 'natural' lives at Marineland to provide a fair indication of their life span in captivity.

Some work has been done on dolphin teeth. Ground down, they show annual layers in the dentine, like the rings in a tree, and it is evident that these could be used

* They are quoted from François Bourlière, *The Natural History of Mammals.*

to establish age; but no extensive sampling of the teeth of aged dolphins has been reported yet, so far as I know.

However, one very great biologist of a former time reported some actual experiments to determine how long dolphins live, made by marking the tails of captured animals. This biologist was Aristotle, and it would seem that these experiments stood alone, and unchallenged, throughout the twenty-three centuries that passed between his lifetime and the founding of Marine Studios. He said, you will remember, that 'fishermen nick their tails sometimes and set them adrift again', and that 'by this expedient' some were known to have lived for 30 years.

That statement is, of course, an important piece of evidence for something else as well. If it is true that the marked animals were identified over such long periods, it establishes that dolphins have what is known as a home range. It is very likely that, like birds, they do not make use of their apparently unlimited freedom to range their element, but stay in one locality throughout their lives – or at any rate return to it each year, as whales are known to do. Some slender evidence for home range in the Bottle-nosed Dolphin of the Florida coast has been reported in the *Journal of Mammalogy*; and we shall hear in Part III of the remarkable New Zealand dolphin Pelorus Jack, which was known to man in one clearly defined locality for twenty-four years. But the greatest credit for information on both these points, home range and life span, still belongs to the greatest biologist of all.

Intelligence and learning

           ○   *○*   *○*   *○*

The time has come to speak of the games that dolphins play and the intelligence they reveal in playing them. Like human children, and puppies and kittens, young dolphins get sensory experience of their environment and also the exercise their growing bodies need by inventing energetic games, in which they display a delightful sense of fun. At times, like human children, they will invent a game that annoys their mother and persist in doing it when she wants them to stop. It is their usual way to do this when she is trying to enjoy a nap.

One young dolphin at Marine Studios in this fashion took to teasing a small turtle. The turtle only wanted to go its own quiet way, but the mischief-maker kept tossing it out of the water with his snout, or trying to roll it like a hoop on the floor of the tank. Another infant took a strong fancy to the youngest of the female dolphins in the tank, and spent hours chasing after her, to the annoyance of its mother, who kept trying to separate them. In both cases the mother showed marvellous patience with her child, and although she was determined to stop the game and recall the young one to her side she never once nipped it or even struck it with her tail. (It seems that mother dolphins never do strike their young.)

Simple chasing seems to be the first stage in a dolphin's play. Then comes teasing, and here we begin to see the animal's mind at work, since in teasing it is usually both acting deliberately and anticipating other actions. One of the young ones at Marineland used to make playful dashes at a pelican floating on the surface. It would seize a feather but would *never bite the pelican*. Another invetend a more deliberate form of teasing: there was a large Red Grouper living in a rock cranny at the bottom of the tank, and the dolphin used to put pieces of squid near the hole and back away, waiting for the ponderous grouper to be tempted. As soon as the grouper came out, the dolphin snatched the bait away.

It was this same animal – his name was Algie, later changed to Algae – who discovered the game of catch-the-feather, using a feather lost by the pelican. He had discovered, perhaps by accident, that if he took it down to one of the sea-water jets at the bottom of the tank and let it go it would race away in the current. Then he would chase it, and he did this again and again. Soon the game was improved on by a female who was two years older than Algae. She released the feather, not in the jet but in the eddy alongside, which gave her time to back away and wait, with her mouth open, until the feather was caught and swept toward her. Later, the two were seen collaborating in this game, each taking a turn to put the feather in while the other waited to catch it.

Algae showed the clearest signs of possessing what we humans would call a personality, and showed them early. His mother was rather unusual. According to Frank S. Essapian (who has described Algae's character in a published article), she was 'lazy, unsociable, and sleepy during the greater part of the day', and Algae quickly took advantage of this. From the age of two weeks he was stealing away from her side while she slept to play with his 'aunts', the younger females in the tank. He was soon their pet, and they seemed to delight in taking him off to play. At the age of two months he was also allowing himself to be touched by the staff (his curiosity having prevailed over an initial, instinctive hesitation) and by then, too, he had begun to play inventively with that principal delight of all the Marineland infant dolphins, an inflated inner tube.

'All the dolphins play with the inner tubes,' Arthur F. McBride and Henry Kritzler write in one of the technical papers which are the sources of this information from Marineland. 'They usually rise up from underneath, spear the rings with their snouts and then, as momentum carries their heads above the surface, hurl the tubes into the air. [Algae] took to this play so readily that at six weeks of age he had already thrown a tube over both rails into the grounds outside. It is significant that only immature dolphins have learned to play fetch, and doubly so that this game was originated by a dolphin, not by its human attendants.'

And Frank Essapian has elsewhere recorded: 'When about a year old, Algae was making jumps out of the water to take fish from the attendant's mouth, a feat that some of the adult porpoises have never undertaken. By the time of his first birthday, two other male porpoises had been born in the tank. Before his second birthday, Algae had become the mainspring of the trio . . . However, it was inevitable that some of his activities would be met with a rebuff from his elders. As a result, Algae bore more cuts, abrasions, and tooth marks than any other porpoise in the tank.'

It is clear that certain of these dolphin games call for something in the nature of thinking ahead, even though the interval of time is very short. In the game of putting the feather in the jet, or teasing the ponderous grouper, the dolphin not only does something, but he *intends* to do something – like the chimpanzees at the Yerkes Laboratories, which, when they see a stranger arrive, will go to the faucet, fill their mouths with water, then sit with innocent faces waiting for the visitor to come within range and be drenched.

Some games among the Marineland dolphins have been developed to the point where three or four join in. A young one in a playful mood may find a feather on the surface; he will balance it on his snout, flip it backward, and try to catch it; then another will dart in to catch the feather as it falls, and race off, chased by others who try to get it from him; one may snatch it from the side of his mouth, and then be pursued by the rest, and so it goes on. To anyone who has never seen dolphins before, this is remarkable enough, but what is even more so is that such games have been known to go on for more than half an hour. Most other animals lose interest in a play pattern long before that.

Sad to say, dolphins, like kittens, become less inclined to play as they grow older. After a few years they too become reserved and dignified. But occasionally, among dolphins as among cats, the childish spirit returns surprisingly, even to the staidest and stiffest of elderly males, and they will join in a game the young ones have begun.

Two things stand out from all this which seem especially significant. One is the unusual mobility of the neck of Bottlenosed Dolphins, a structural characteristic of the species which surely has contributed something to their unusually 'human' character. Their personalities are anything but stiff-necked. The other is the observation of McBride and Kritzler that the game of fetch was 'originated by a dolphin, not by its human attendants'.

This is fully borne out by Forrest G. Wood, Jr, who is Director of Exhibits at Marineland now (and successor to Mr McBride and Dr Kritzler). We think of dogs as animals that can be taught to do tricks, and probably people who have seen the dolphins at Marineland think of them in the same way. According to Forrest Wood, it would be truer to say that the dolphins have learned that human beings can be taught to do tricks. 'All of the younger animals that were born in the tank have become adept at this,' he wrote in *Mariner* in 1954. 'They have found that if they toss the rubber ring to someone standing at the rail, that person will quickly learn to throw it back, and will continue the game until the porpoise tires of it. That two creatures of such unlike habit and habitat have learned to share an activity that yields mutual enjoyment speaks well, I think, for both porpoise and man.'

And what if the human should tire of the game before the animal? In that case the dolphin will show its impatience in the plainest manner by putting its head out of the water and making a high-pitched grating noise from its blowhole, until the human throws the ring again and the game is resumed.

Thus by invention and imitation (or reinvention), by handing on from old to young and from one generation to the next, the dolphin colony at Marineland has evolved in play the beginnings of a 'culture' of its own creation. And so no doubt did the remote ancestors of the human species begin to evolve from equally simple beginnings our own

culture of work and play, which ranges by now from playing with our own bath toys in infancy to making scientific
studies of dolphins playing with theirs.

From the deliberate teasing of the grouper, and from
the game of putting the feather beside the water jet, it is
clear that young dolphins are capable of having an *intention* (which is not unique, however; many other animals
exhibit comparable behaviour). From the way they im-
prove upon their games it is clear that they are capable
of *developing* an idea. And from the fact that they will go
on playing for half an hour or more without human
encouragement, it is clear that they are capable of *sustained
interest*. All this suggests that the dolphin is, indeed, a
highly intelligent animal, like the dog, or even more like
the chimpanzee. And the point that would seem to clinch
the matter is their possession of something that psychologists call *insight*.

Dolphins can go one better than developing and sustain-
ing a game they have discovered by chance. They can
work out a way of doing something when the way is not
immediately obvious, or in other words they can solve a
problem. Here is an example, given by McBride and
Kritzler. A young female was playing fetch one day with
a wet pelican feather, throwing it repeatedly to a human
playmate at the side of the tank. On one of her throws the
feather failed to clear the rail, and stuck to the wall above
water level. She could not pick it off with her mouth
because of the way her chin protrudes below her upper
jaw. 'She neatly solved the problem,' McBride records,
'by rising above water level and wiping the feather back
into the water with the side of her head, there to pick it
up and resume the game.' Having found that it worked,

she used the same method afterwards, when the feather became stuck again.

Even more impressive was the performance in later years of a dolphin that located a piece of dead squid (put in as food for the turtles), which had drifted out of reach under a bridge of rock. 'The dolphin swam forward over the bridge,' writes F. G. Wood, Jr, 'and swept her tail flukes sharply downward, thus "blowing" the squid from under the rock.' *

Animal intelligence is hard to define, and harder still to measure. It is difficult enough to make comparisons between different human races, and infinitely more so between different animal species, and no one has yet devised any system of tests in which the same yardstick can be applied to animals of widely different habits or bodily forms. How would a dolphin, which has virtually no limbs, compete in tests with the chimpanzee, which uses its hands so cleverly?

Of course, the fact that they are gregarious animals greatly helps the dolphins to reveal their intelligence to us, as it does the chimpanzees. Being social animals by nature they are accustomed to co-operating in the wild, and to having a leader to whom they are in some degree subservient. To be *able* to take part in games and do tricks is one thing, to be *willing* is another, and it is the habit of co-operation, even more than intelligence, that determines whether an animal will play or work with human beings. It is for this reason that dogs, horses, and elephants have

* Described to the author in a letter by Mr Wood, who later adds, however: 'I was indeed impressed by this, but . . . must consider the possibility that the animal learned to do this by accident, but remembered and continued to use the technique, which is also rather impressive.'

become the useful servants of man that they are, and cats, on the other hand, although intelligent, will not co-operate to anything like the same extent – since in their wild state they live a solitary life, hunting alone, and not working with others, and in particular not having a boss to their social group.

The ability to learn, then, in itself is not necessarily a sign of intelligence, nor is quickness necessarily a measure of it (even an earthworm can quickly learn a simple 'don't'). Nor can it be said that willingness in itself is the proof of the matter (though obviously there is a strong connection between intelligence and the social habit). In short, if we are considering intelligence alone, it is not the fact of being *able* to learn that distinguishes the higher animals from the lower, but the *kind* of learning they are capable of, and whether they can carry it any further; and whether they can solve a problem by insight.

It is necessary to remember that there are two ways in which an animal can solve a problem. One is by fumbling at it repeatedly, getting successes by accident and eventually learning to do the right thing without necessarily understanding it. The other is by grasping the principle of it, whether quickly or not. (It is obvious that *speed* in achieving success may be misleading; it may be accidental in the trial-and-error method, and irrelevant in the second.)

Dolphins in their play have shown signs of solving problems in the second manner. They have done things that require a form of thinking – the stuck pelican feather, the piece of squid under the rock. And although no fully acceptable tests of their intelligence have yet been made, there is reason to believe they would perform very well if practicable tests could be devised.*

There is also the physical evidence of their brain – its size, and the way in which certain parts of it have been developed. Just as the size and complexity of an electrical switchboard may indicate to an expert how much goes on in a certain building, and the relative importance of the various circuits, so can the size and structure of an animal's brain give hints about its intelligence and the development of its various senses. (In the brain of a dog, for instance, the olfactory bulbs are large, whereas in the dolphin they are not discernible.)

The Bottlenosed Dolphin has a large brain, so large that in proportion to body length it runs a close second to the brain of man. For each foot of body length, *Homo sapiens* has about eight and a half ounces of brain and *Tursiops truncatus* has just under seven; the gorilla, our nearest anthropoid cousin, has on the same basis only about three ounces. In absolute terms (which are irrelevant here, but they help us to picture the thing of which we are speaking) a *Tursiops* brain is about half again as big as that of a man. It weighs about three and three-quarter pounds (for a body that may weigh 400 pounds).

The cerebrum, its most important part, is large in the same proportion. This is the large 'new' part that crowds over the rest of the brain in the higher animals, especially in the monkeys, the chimpanzees, and man himself. As to the various senses – of smell, touch, sight, and hearing – the nerve connections of a dolphin's brain show exactly

* The foregoing paragraphs are greatly indebted to but rather freely summarised from the 1948 paper on dolphin behaviour of McBride and D. O. Hebb.

what they might be expected to: that there is not much sense of smell, if any at all, and the sense of touch is little used; but the sight nerve is relatively large, and the hearing nerve is larger still, indicating special development of the auditory sense; likewise, the areas of the brain that receive these nerves reflect the same thing.

Some curious work in connection with the dolphin brain has been done in Florida in the last few years by John C. Lilly, a neurophysiologist who became interested in the dolphins at Marineland and has since constructed, with financial help from the United States Navy, an experimental station at Nazareth Bay, St Thomas, in the Virgin Islands.

Dr Lilly has had a good deal of publicity for his work. He has been reported throughout the world (incorrectly, one would hope) as saying that on the evidence of its brain the Bottlenosed Dolphin may be man's intellectual equal. He does believe that dolphins may prove to be even more intelligent than we can see them to be at present, and he is attempting to establish communication with them as sentient beings; he is trying to talk to them, and to get them to talk to him.

He reasons, plausibly, that if men are going to be sent into space it would be valuable to acquire some experience *now* in communicating with creatures that inhabit a radically different environment from our own and have a large brain – and which, incidentally, know something of the weightlessness that man will experience in space. This is not his only approach to the question of dolphin intelligence. Dr Lilly has been using the dolphin for certain experiments for which, he says, it is eminently fitted not only by the large size of its brain but also by the gentleness of its nature. It is the only animal with a brain the size of ours 'who will co-operate and not frighten me to the point where I can't work with him'. And so he has been inserting electrodes into dolphins' brains (they do not hurt, and the insertion is done with a local anaesthetic) in order to investigate those areas that are concerned – as it appears they are – with positive, pleasure, or reward feelings, and those concerned with negative, or 'pain' feelings. I am paraphrasing now from Dr Lilly's 1958 paper, which he kindly sent me, titled *Some Considerations Regarding Basic Mechanisms of Positive and Negative Types of Motivation.* It has been known for some time that there are zones of the brain in monkeys, rats, and men which are concerned with what I shall loosely call the 'no' feelings, and larger zones concerned with the 'yes' feelings, and that these zones can be electrically stimulated with resultant distress or pleasure to the animal. Requiring a large-brained beast with a peaceable temperament, Dr Lilly finds the gentle dolphin ideal for his tests; and so, in the Virgin Islands, where it is warm enough to work in the open all the year round and with the United States Navy sufficiently in-terested to meet part of the cost, he is sticking little wires into the heads of dolphins fetched in fibreglass cradles from Marineland, and is getting them to switch the current on and off themselves.

One wild dolphin, freshly captured, learned to work the yes switch after something like twenty uncannily purpose-ful tries, against the hundreds of random tries a monkey took to achieve the same result. Dr Lilly's dolphins have even begun to 'talk', after a fashion. That is to say, they have made certain noises which Dr Lilly considers were attempts to mimic sounds they associated with the attaining of gratification. As a result, Dr Lilly (according to *Time* magazine) 'is now convinced that they have an extremely complicated language'. One animal, when the current was cut off (making gratification unattainable), 'immediately stopped working and vocalised – apparently scolding at times, and mimicking us at others'. He mimicked Dr Lilly's voice so well that Mrs Lilly laughed out loud, and he copied that as well.

A caution is needed here, lest such behaviour be considered proof of intelligence: imitation which in a parrot would be labelled 'parrot-fashion' does not necessarily become something else when it suddenly occurs, or appears to occur, in a large-brained aquatic mammal.*

The ending of this story of Dr Lilly's is in the Greek tradition. For this dolphin, which had come so willingly so close to human intercourse, eventually perished for the act. He 'pushed too rapidly', says Lilly, 'caused a seizure, became unconscious, respiration failed, and he died'.

Although I do hope that such fatalities can be avoided in the future, I think we can look forward with the liveliest expectation to the further outcome of Dr Lilly's experiments with the gentle *Tursiops*.

I have said enough now of the dolphin's intelligence and its brain, but have not quite finished with the question of where it stands in the hierarchy of the 'higher' animals, in what D. O. Hebb calls the phylogenetic scale. Apart from

* And F. G. Wood, Jr, writes in a letter to the author: 'Observing and listening to porpoises over the years, none of us at Marineland has ever detected any indication that a porpoise was attempting to reproduce a sound it heard, though they can undoubtedly hear the announcers' voices over the public address system repeating the same words during the feeding programme six times a day, and the same music preceding each programme.'

displays of mere intelligence, there are certain other elements of their behaviour, concerned with their emotions rather than their wits, which in Hebb's view would support the dolphin's claim to a high position among the higher animals.

Some years ago, when two full-grown males were living together in the tank at Marineland and had grown used to each other (in contrast to what usually happens with a pair of males), one of them was taken away to be exhibited in another place. After a three-week absence it was brought back, and when it was released in the tank the other male showed great excitement. Arthur F. McBride, the curator of Marine Studios at that time, describes what happened: 'No doubt could exist that the two recognised each other, and for several hours they swam side by side, rushing frenziedly through the water, and on several occasions they leaped completely out of the water. For several days, the two males were inseparable, and neither paid any attention to the female.' The fact that this occurred in the courting season made it the more remarkable.

This capacity for an individual attachment, Hebb points out, is totally unlike anything seen in the rat. Dogs have it a little, chimpanzees far more so, and humans in great degree. And so the behaviour of the reunited animals may class the dolphin 'with the chimpanzee rather than with the dog'.

Another dolphin characteristic which Hebb places in this category is that of entertaining fears – for more than a brief time – of unfamiliar inanimate objects. The captive dolphins (I quote from McBride and Hebb) 'react in a characteristic way to strange objects in the tank'. They gather in a tight school as far from the object as possible and swim in unison. If it turns out after all to be something that they know (such as the raft occasionally used in the tank), the school breaks up. If it is something new, and especially if it is something big like a seine, 'they will remain schooled and swim excitedly in a tight pack', with loud and frequent whistling. In an hour or two, if the object is motionless or flows with the current in the tank, they will get back to normal; but the object itself they may avoid for some days. This again is more like the behaviour of the chimpanzee than that of the dog.

Two other remarkable pieces of dolphin behaviour which support all this have been recorded since McBride and Hebb studied the subject. They come from Marine Studios' sister institution in California, Marineland of the Pacific. I am quoting the descriptions not from a popular magazine but from the unimpeachable pages of the *Journal of Mammalogy*, from a paper by David H. Brown and Kenneth S. Norris.

The first, which the authors merely describe as 'tempting but difficult to interpret', occurred on October 25, 1954, when two Bottlenosed Dolphins were trying to haul a Moray Eel out of its rock crevice on the bottom of the tank:

'One dolphin was on each side of the crevice working the moray back and forth. They could not dislodge the eel. One dolphin left the scene, killed a newly introduced scorpion fish (*Scorpaena guttata*) and returned to the crevice with the fish in his mouth. The scorpion fish is a species with sharp and painfully poisonous dorsal spines. The *Tursiops* poked at the eel with this fish, apparently prodding it with the spines. The eel abandoned its crevice, was caught, and taken to the middle of the tank and released.'

In the face of the authors' own commendable reserve, it would be impudent to yield to the temptation to interpret this remarkable incident in any way. Let us turn then to the other example. It concerns, for a change, a pair of Common Dolphins, *Delphinus delphis*, and is in fact the first story in this book where *Delphinus*' identity is established beyond all doubt.*

In July 1954 (Brown and Norris write) a small female *Delphinus* was captured by means of a hook, placed in a holding tank, and given the name Pauline. She was in a state of shock and could not keep herself afloat. Adrenalin injections made no difference, so a set of waterwings was made for her: four large glass jars were attached to her sides as floats. No one expected to find her alive next morning, but in fact she was. For two days she floated helplessly about, and would probably have died except for the fact that on the third day the collectors brought in a 'fine large male *Delphinus*'. He immediately sought the company of the afflicted Pauline, who, 'in a matter of seconds, indicated by her movements her willingness to associate with her own kind, and made some effort to swim'. The bottles were removed, and she began to labour slowly round the tank. The male sometimes swam under her and nudged her to the surface. Gradually she recovered, and the two animals 'became inseparable'. But

* In the classical tales, the dolphins could be either *Delphinus* or *Tursiops*. At Marine Studios the exhibit has been confined to animals common off the Florida coast (*Tursiops* and the Spotted Dolphin). In California, *Delphinus* has proved the least adjusted dolphin in captivity, being timid and having little tendency to play – the opposite of its nature in the wild.

two months later Pauline died. She was found to have a large abscess under the scar tissue of her hook wound, which had healed on the outside when cleansed and treated with sulpha drugs. She died on September 8.

At the time of her death the male circled her body, 'whistling constantly'. He then refused all food, and after three days of ceaseless swimming round and round the tank, whistling most of the time, he also died. Examination, as Brown and Norris record without a tear and without a smile, 'revealed the presence of a perforated gastric ulcer. This ulcerous condition was probably aggravated by the animal's refusal to feed, resulting in a perforation, the ensuing peritonitis and death. Healed gastric ulcers have since been found in two other specimens examined in our laboratory. The primary cause of these ulcers was not determined . . .'

Pliny or Plutarch would not have hesitated to say that Pauline's mourner died of grief. If science insists that their view is untenable – what a pity!

Intelligence, then, with success in problem-solving and some evidence of 'insight'; a capacity for sustained interest and sustained fears; moods and emotions that last for long periods; a capacity for 'friendship' of a nonbiological kind, and some sexual versatility, not of the crude type found in lower animals; fears that suggest 'imagination'; a certain ingenuity (if Brown and Norris will permit the term) with regard to the moray and the scorpion fish; a touching devotion to the afflicted, a profound capacity for grief, even to the point of pining away from 'sorrow and regret'. All these things add up to suggest fairly strongly that the dolphins should be placed very high in the hierarchy of the beasts; certainly somewhere in the region of the dogs and the chimpanzees, and possibly (if Dr Lilly is right) above the latter, which is to say in the 'highest' position next to man himself.

But this conclusion, now so elaborately deduced thanks chiefly to the work of McBride and Hebb, was long ago arrived at by an insight of that ancient pioneer of animal psychology – a Greek, of course – the fabulist Aesop. It was some two hundred years before the time of Aristotle, and 2500 years before the time of McBride and Hebb and Lilly, that Aesop told this story of 'The Monkey and the Dolphin'.

'It was an old custom among sailors to carry about with them little Maltese lap-dogs, or Monkeys, to amuse them on the voyage; so it happened once upon a time that a man took with him a Monkey as a companion on board ship. While they were off Sunium, the famous promontory of Attica, the ship was caught in a violent storm, and being capsized, all on board were thrown in the water, and had to swim for land as best they could. And among them was the Monkey. A Dolphin saw him struggling, and, taking him for a man, went to his assistance and bore him on his back straight for shore. When they had just got opposite Piraeus, the harbour of Athens, the Dolphin asked the Monkey "if he were an Athenian?" "Yes", answered the Monkey, "assuredly, and of one of the first families in the place." "Then, of course, you know Piraeus," said the Dolphin. "Oh, yes," said the Monkey, who thought it was the name of some distinguished citizen, "he is one of my most intimate friends." Indignant at so gross a deceit and falsehood, the Dolphin dived at once to the bottom, and left the lying Monkey to his fate.'

It seems a pity that Dr Lilly could not conduct his communication experiments in the eastern Mediterranean instead of the Caribbean Sea, and so take advantage of the dolphins' familiarity with Greek – the original, and in some ways still the only, language of disinterested science.

If it is true that dolphins are helpful to one another, and also intelligent, and of a gentle nature – even 'kind' – is it true that they have purposely saved human beings from drowning? I do not think it is. But this is not to say that no one has ever been saved from drowning by a dolphin's *actions*, nor am I saying that the stories of Arion and Hermias were untrue. On the contrary, a personal account has been published in our own times, in *Natural History* magazine, of an indubitable rescue incident.

It happened in 1943, on the coast of Florida, to the wife of an attorney who was bathing from a private beach, alone. She had gone in only waist-deep when she realised there was a strong undertow, and before she could get back to shore the undertow pulled her down. She was frightened, swallowed some water, and began to lose consciousness – desperately wishing as she did so that someone would push her back. 'With that,' she afterwards wrote, 'someone gave me a tremendous shove.' She landed on the shore, too exhausted to turn round and express her thanks to her rescuer. When she did turn round, no one at all was there; but a few yards out from the shore a dolphin was leaping around, and beyond it another creature, leaping too. A man who had seen the last part of the incident then came running over. He told the woman that when he first saw her in the water she 'looked like a dead body', and that the dolphin had shoved her ashore. He described the other creature, probably in error, as a shark.

Was the dolphin really 'helping' the drowning woman – that is, deliberately assisting what it knew to be a creature in distress? Or was it merely adding to the fun of its own game with the other dolphin (as the other creature presumably was)? We know from Marineland now, as well as from Aristotle, that a mother dolphin will support her 'little dead one' at the surface long after it has ceased to breathe; but this could be explained as an instinctive behaviour pattern concerned with survival of the species, something a 'lower' animal would do as well, and not involving high intelligence. By some, the dolphin's natural playfulness and curiosity have been held to offer all the necessary explanation for reported human rescues; and it has been pointed out that dolphins have also been seen working hard to push a water-logged mattress ashore. There is more to the matter than this. Adult dolphins have been seen co-operating in the ocean to support an *adult* companion in distress,* and one especially interesting case is reported in the pages of the *Journal of Mammalogy*, by J. B. Siebenaler and D. K. Caldwell.

On October 30, 1954, a boat was collecting specimens for the Florida aquarium 'The Living Sea', at Walton Beach. A stick of dynamite was exploded under water near a school of two dozen *Tursiops*, and one of them was stunned. It began to race around the vessel with a 45-degree list, but almost at once two other adults came to its aid. They swam up from below, one on either side, and placed their heads under its flippers to keep it afloat. Unable to breathe like that, they had to break away from time to time, and it *appeared* that another pair then took their place (but the water was rough, and the observers could not be sure it wasn't the first pair back again). The whole school remained nearby until the stunned one

* It has also become a commonplace in captivity.

recovered – several minutes after the explosion – and then made off at high speed with great exultant leaps in unison.

This does lend credence to the rescue story, and to a degree that the mother-infant behaviour cannot be said to, though the distinction between the motivations is extremely fine. Preventing the death of an adult of the species is much the same, from the survival viewpoint, as preventing the death of an infant. As for the wife of an attorney – *she* is something entirely different, and to a dolphin perhaps may not have much more meaning than a mattress.

Whatever may be the truth about all this, sailors for many centuries have firmly believed that dolphins may save them from drowning in case of shipwreck, and also that they will protect them from sharks by surrounding them and driving the sharks away. This latter idea is much more easily explained. Certain species of shark are natural enemies of the dolphin, and should it happen that both are present at a scene of trouble it would be natural for the dolphins, if they outnumber the sharks, to drive them off; and the next thing we know, there is another 'rescue' story to the dolphin's credit.

So the woman on the Florida beach was 'helped' in some way certainly and Arion of the legend, too, I think – if not quite in the way he afterwards said (we must remember that Arion was a poet). And considering how much devotion the dolphins show to one another, not only to their infants but to their adult comrades in distress, it is no loss to their reputation if their human rescues have not been deliberate.

Dolphins are mammals, and mammals, it is often said,

are the most successful of all the animal groups. They have contrived to live in every sort of environment, from the tropical jungle to the polar wastes: they thrive on plains and mountains, in forests and deserts, in marshes and meadows, in solitude and cities. The smallest mammal is a tiny shrew, the largest a hundred-foot whale, the largest creature that has ever lived. There are mammals that can run, jump, crawl, burrow, swim on the water and under it, and glide and fly. And if the cleverest of all mammals is man himself, the most excellent among the others is surely the dolphin.

It is remarkable enough that the dolphins, whose ancestors once had legs and hair and delivered and suckled their young on land, can now complete their whole life cycle under water and outswim the superbly streamlined fishes whose ancestors never left the element at all. Their breathing and suckling arrangements, the modification of their skin for speed, and their development of echo-location (which I am coming to in the next chapter) are marvellous examples of the mammal's capacity to adapt. Then what of their intelligence in this context? How has it been developed in the marine environment, and why, and to what end?

The cetaceans have lived in the sea, cut off from contact with all other mammals (save man himself, occasionally, and the seals) for sixty million years or more. In all that time, unlike the apes, the dogs, the cats and the elephants and horses, they have not had the experience of sharing their environment with other intelligent or semi-intelligent animals. For company, as for diet, they have had only the fishes. Yet they appear to match the higher animals in intelligence. We do not know, of course, what degree of intelligence the dolphins' ancestors took with them when they returned to the sea, or how it has been developed or adapted since. If it was high, it does not seem to have slipped back; if it was low, it has advanced. How has it managed to do that in the sea, and (which is really the same question) what part has it played in the whole development of the animal?

To go right back to the start, intelligence depends in the first place on the development of the cerebral cortex, and the capacity for this to develop was inherent in the layout of the mammalian brain. (The same is not true of the fishes.) After that it depends on 'selection pressure'. If intelligence is an advantage to an animal, the animal will develop it further. Admittedly, the more competition there is with other semi-intelligent animals present, the more advantage intelligence will be. But the absence of contact with other mammals is not a real difficulty. The very intelligence of the dolphin in fact would seem to indicate that it is not a question of the company one keeps, and that the sea offers just as many opportunities for the use of intelligence as any other environment.*

* At this point I cannot resist appending an unscientific but delightfully relevant passage from *On the Cleverness of Animals*, showing how Plutarch approached the same question:

'The land is wide open for investigation by the senses. The sea, on the other hand, grants us but a few dubious glimpses. She draws a veil over the birth and growth, the attacks and reciprocal defences, of most of her denizens. Among these there are no few feats of intelligence and memory and community spirit that remain unknown to us and so obstruct our argument [i.e., "whether land or sea animals are cleverer"]. Then too, land animals by reason of their close relationship and their cohabitation have to some extent been imbued with human manners; they have the advantage of their breeding and teaching and imitation, which sweetens all their bitterness and sullenness, like fresh water mixed with brine, while their lack of understanding and dullness are roused to life by human contacts. Whereas

In the early stages of the cetaceans' aquatic evolution it may well have offered more. When they were presumably less well adapted, intelligent use of the new environment would have been at a high premium. There is nothing like living at a bare subsistence level for sharpening the wits.

Then there is the question (I should really have put it first) whether the environment is simple or complex in terms of sensory experience. The particular value of the cerebral cortex in the higher animals is in storing up and cataloguing a large amount of information about a wide variety of sensory experiences, and if the environment were not a varied one, and the conditions were extremely uniform, there would be little advantage in having a complex brain to deal with it. The animals from which the apes, monkeys, and man are descended dwelt in the trees; and it has been said, incidentally, that the three-dimensional character of this environment may well have been important in the development of their intelligence. Human beings now live in an environment certainly complex and under conditions certainly not uneventful (since it is a tendency of ours to make quite certain they do not become so), and from our own or Plutarch's standpoint the sea might appear to be just the opposite. But the underwater swimmers, with their cameras and colour film, are speedily changing this opinion.

---

the life of sea creatures, being set apart by mighty bounds from intercourse with men and having nothing adventitious or acquired from human usage, is peculiar to itself, indigenous, and uncontaminated by foreign ways, not by distinction of Nature, but of location. For their nature is such as to welcome and retain such instruction as reaches them. This it is that renders many eels tractable, like those that are called sacred in Arethusa . . .'

There is no lack of the unexpected in the sea. Other animals, fast or sluggish, threatening or not, can loom up out of the blue, and there is obviously a tremendous difference in terms of sensation between the surface waters and the depths; and the three-dimensional range itself, like the apes' environment in the trees, may have been important for the cetaceans. Here, by the way, we find an interesting connection between the animal's psychology and its structure. If the three-dimensional environment *has* meant as much to the cetaceans as it probably has to the primates, it is worth recalling the three-dimensional character (from the locomotion standpoint) of the dolphin tail – the tail that happens to give the animal such excellent lateral mobility in addition to the vertical movement for which it is primarily adapted. Fishes, in so far as their structure makes no ideal provision for movement up and down, may be said to live on planes within the sea, and the same is true to a certain extent of most mammals on the land – but not of the primates. Which all comes down to saying something like this: as in the forest, so in the green pathways of the sea, life possesses an extra dimension for those fitted both to perceive it and to respond to it in their behaviour. And this extra dimension may have had much to do with developing the intelligence of the dolphins.

Finally, there is the question of the cetaceans' own social nature. The interaction within the species between one individual and another, and between one individual and the group, provides an additional and very large source of sensory experience. Since it is impossible to say which comes first, intelligence or the social nature, and since cats are intelligent without being social and rabbits are social without being intelligent, perhaps this question is better left alone!

At all events, it would seem that intelligence may have played an important part in the success of the dolphins in the sea. Just how important is for the biologists and psychologists to work out between them, if they can.

Dolphin hearing

Everything that is known about dolphins nowadays is so interesting that it is difficult to know what to mention first. It is time to talk of the sounds they make, and of the purpose of these sounds.

You will remember that Oppian, when describing the night-fishing on the coast of Euboea, says that the dolphins leapt at the mullet like dogs, 'answering bark with bark'. It is perfectly true that dolphins make yelping noises when they are very excited – though not with their mouths open, like dogs. The staff at Marine Studios have heard them doing it, and by keeping watch, and listening to them with an underwater microphone, they have discovered that the Bottlenosed Dolphins have many different noises, possibly with different meanings.*

* A gramophone record of some of these sounds has been issued by Marine Studios, and another is available in the Folkways Records series.

Noises, in fact, are so important to dolphins that you might say their sense of hearing is to them what seeing is to us. We live in a world of sights and sounds, and most of us would say that sight comes first, although in fact it doesn't (we hear a noise, and look round to see what made it; and when we are asleep, it is our ears, not our eyes, that tell us there is a burglar in the house). Nevertheless, and though a deaf man would not agree, we live in what we feel is a pre-eminently visual world; the dolphin lives in an emphatically aural world. For him, much more than for us, sound comes first and sight comes after. When a dolphin thinks of a particular place in the sea – in so far as a dolphin may be said to think – he probably thinks of the noises that are heard there, the snapping of the shrimps, the rolling of the pebbles, the sounds made by the particular fishes that live in that spot; and when he thinks of his mate, he probably thinks of her voice rather than what she looks like. Moreover, when he hears a noise he can tell exactly what direction it is coming from. So when he wants to find his mate, or his mother, he doesn't *look* for her, he listens. Excellent though his eyes are, he cannot see far unless the water is unusually clear; instead, he can form an impression of his surroundings through his sense of hearing. And this applies, as we shall see, not only to things in the sea that make their own noises, but also to inanimate objects like rocks, and the sea bottom itself, and floating objects that the dolphin needs to avoid.

One of the commonest noises made by Bottlenosed Dolphins is a kind of whistling. It can be 'seen' as well as heard, since a stream of little bubbles comes from the blowhole when they do it. They whistle when they are playing, or even when they are merely cruising round; and if something strange excites them, then they all start whistling. It is whistling that enables them to keep together as a family and as a school. The babies start to whistle as soon as they are born, and like lambs they can recognise their mother's call soon afterwards. At Marine Studios, if a mother and her baby are accidentally separated (for instance by the gates that close the channel connecting the two main tanks) they will whistle to each other through the water. On one occasion when this happened, the mother remained circling about the spot where her infant had last been with her, whistling until they were reunited. On another occasion it was the infant that stayed in one place, whistling until its mother was able to return.

At feeding times the Marine Studios dolphins make a variety of mewing and rasping sounds. At mealtimes, too, there is sometimes heard a loud jaw clap, not unlike the sound of clapping hands. It is often used by the bull, who has a rather bossy nature, as a sound of intimidation; females sometimes use it to express their displeasure at unwanted male approaches; nursing mothers use it when another animal interferes with their young; and the young themselves use it at times, producing a rather feeble clap at first but improving with practice.

These noises are all what might be called communication sounds – sounds that dolphins make to find one another, to keep in touch, or merely to express their feelings. Some of them are 'language' noises, in the sense that a dog's growling is language, and all of them are meant to go from one dolphin to another, or to many others. These are the sounds Dr Lilly is hoping to translate into English. But aside from these the dolphins possess a separate repertoire of sounds of a special character by which they can locate an object in the water even though it makes no sound of its own.

Bats, as is now well known, have a system of echo-location which works in the same way as radar, except that it uses sound waves instead of radio waves. Before radar was invented it was known that bats could 'see' in the dark, by sending out high-frequency sounds or ultrasounds, and picking up the echo from solid objects in their path. Under the name of ASDIC, a similar device was developed for underwater use in World War II. And within the last few years it has been established that the Bottlenosed Dolphin employs echo-location too.

The reason I specify *Tursiops* here is that the same has not yet been proved for those other species that live farther out to sea. Bottlenosed Dolphins live in coastal waters – or, as Oppian would say, 'they rejoice in the echoing shores'. These waters are murkier than the open sea and also contain more obstacles; therefore coastal dolphins have greater need of sound-as-sight than dolphins living farther out. And at Marine Studios it has been noticed that the Spotted Dolphin, *Stenella plagiodon*, which is an offshore variety, makes far less sound of all kinds than *Tursiops*. (It also has a smaller repertoire; only two different sounds have been recorded from *Stenella*.)

The first hint that dolphins might have echo-location, or sonar, was given some years ago, when one of the Marine Studios fishermen noticed that, if they were using an ordinary small-meshed seine to capture mullet or other small fish in the sea and dolphins were present, the dolphins would never charge into the net; instead, they would leap over the cork line to escape, and they would do this even at night and in murky water. On the other hand, the dolphins would invariably charge into a net of larger mesh (with holes about ten inches square). It was as if they could 'see' the small net in the water, but not the larger one, or only dimly.* Under the conditions in which this happened they could not have been seeing it with their eyes. The only time a dolphin would jump over a wide-meshed net was after others had struck it and had momentarily pulled the cork line under water.

When this happened (wrote A. F. McBride), 'a dolphin not already caught in the net recognises that what was formerly a solid barrier now has an opening. He promptly rolls over the net where the cork line is lowest. On one of the occasions I have observed this, the night was pitch dark and the dolphin who escaped was not swimming close to the net. He streaked for the low spot in a flash, rolled over it, and was gone.' McBride guessed that the dolphins might be detecting the presence of the fine net, and even of the large-mesh net, by echo-location. Since some of the dolphin sounds that were heard in the tanks at Marine Studios were unexplained, perhaps this was their purpose? In 1956, two experimenters working at the Woods Hole Oceanographic Institution in Massachusetts showed fairly clearly that it was, and later research at Florida State University has proved it conclusively.

The principle used in animal sonar is now so widely understood, thanks to its use in radar, that it scarcely needs explaining. The animal emits a series of sounds that include some overtones of very high pitch and the echoes bounce back to him from any objects that are in the way.

* 'Indications are that the porpoise net (mesh 9 or 10 in. square) is near the limit of resolution for the animals' sonar. They apparently *can* detect it, but get such a weak signal that they can be stampeded into it.' (Forrest Wood's note.)

By practice (which has been acquired unconsciously) he can then tell how far away and in what direction the object is. There is nothing mysterious or superhuman about this, for we ourselves already use the faculty in a cruder way, as, for instance, when we seem to 'sense' the nearness of a wall or a lamp-post in the dark, or when a blind man orients himself to his unseen surroundings by the tapping noises of his stick; and dolphins in the sea, like bats in the dark, have merely sharpened the faculty to the point where it has become a precision instrument. A dolphin makes certain noises (they are thought to be produced somewhere in the nasal passages) that contain both low-pitched sounds such as we ourselves can hear, and very high-pitched sounds, or ultrasounds; and from the returning echoes he can build up a sort of 'picture' of his surroundings as man now does with the help of radar. In particular, he can locate a fish in the dark or in murky water and swoop upon it as accurately as if he could see it. He can even tell how big it is, and this has been seen on the television screen – a blindfold dolphin choosing the fish he wants by its size.

The first *reported* experiments* to establish all this were done in a pond at the Woods Hole Oceanographic Institution by William E. Schevill and Barbara Lawrence, using an old bull *Tursiops* which had been flown there from Marine Studios. The pond was about a hundred yards long and murky, and there was nothing in it for the dolphin to eat, but he very soon learned that on hearing certain signals he would be given a butterfish (which was dead but fresh). By watching him and using a hydrophone, or

* W. N. Kellogg's work (see below), though published later, was begun earlier.

underwater microphone, to listen to him, the experimenters discovered how he worked. It happened that an injury had blinded his right eye, and this helped their tests.

The sound that all the Marineland dolphins respond to best as a call to food is that made by slapping the water with the hand or with a fish. This is the natural sound of leaping mullet, and is something that dolphins already associate with food if they have lived in the wild. So the experimenters began by calling their dolphin in this way. They found that, wherever he was at the time, he could always tell exactly where the sound had been made and came directly to the spot. He appeared to know, within inches, where the slap had been made, even from sixty feet away. This showed that with his *ordinary* hearing (used for noises made in the water by other things) he had an extremely sharp sense of both direction and range. But his ordinary hearing was not what they were interested in; they wanted to know how he located an object that made no noise, and whether he did so by emitting sounds of his own. As a first step toward this they taught him to answer two signals, which could be made at some distance from the feeding punt. One they made by striking an iron pipe suspended in the water, and the other was an ultrasound, produced electronically by an oscillator. The dolphin soon learned that whenever one of these signals was given there would be a fish waiting for him in the water, probably at the feeding punt.

Then they began to try him out. They made a signal but did not put the fish in the water, or they put it where he wasn't expecting it to be. They found that on hearing the signal he would show interest and would approach the feeding platform, but if the fish was not in the water he would swim on past. If the fish was then silently slipped in he would turn back, just as if he had 'seen' it over his shoulder. Sometimes, when he had not been told by signal to expect a fish, he would detect it for himself – but not by vision. In all these tests the experimenters were satisfied he was not seeing the fish with his eye, either because the water was too murky, or because it was night time, or because he had his blind eye toward the platform. However, when it was possible he did use his good eye for the final check.

Through the hydrophone and an amplifier Mr Schevill and Miss Lawrence listened to the sounds that the dolphin himself was making to give him his echoes; and here at last was discovered the explanation of a certain sound that had often been heard at Marine Studios. It was known there as the 'rusty hinge' noise, because it sounded like a door swinging on an old dry hinge. It consisted in fact of hundreds of tiny clicks, close together. (This had been ascertained by recording it and playing back at slow speed.) At Marine Studios the dolphins usually made this noise when examining anything new and strange in the water, such as the hydrophone itself, but there were always so many other noises and distractions in the tank that no one could definitely establish its purpose. At Woods Hole, where the dolphin was alone in the pond and the pond was free from noise, it became plain that the rusty-hinge noise was being used for echo-location.

The experimenters found that when the dolphin was 'creaking' he would nearly always head straight for the fish, even though it had been slipped into the water without a sound and without enough movement for him to see.

If he wasn't creaking, his aim was not so good. Moreover, he would sometimes circle the pond, creaking only as he passed the feeding platform. When he was homing on the target in the last few feet, he wagged his head from side to side, in time with the creaking. It became evident that by doing this he could locate the fish accurately from a distance of up to fifteen feet.

The result of this work was published in 1956; but the study was begun and has since been taken much farther by W. N. Kellogg, Professor of Experimental Psychology at Florida State University. He has already described the results of his nine years' research far better than I can, in his book *Porpoises and Sonar*, but with his permission and for the sake of making these pages complete in themselves, I shall briefly describe them again.

As a first step, Dr Kellogg and two colleagues analysed the acoustic properties of the creaking noise, and found that the clicks that composed it fully satisfied the requirements for echo-location by what is called the pulse-modulation method. (The returning echoes would make a pattern with their originals in the dolphin's hearing, by either alternating or overlapping with them; for instance, given a click one thousandth of a second in length and a fish just two and a half feet from the dolphin's head, the start of the echo would join up with the end of its original.) This was in 1952. Six years later Kellogg was able to report the results of a series of fascinating experiments that went much further than the intervening ones of Schevill and Lawrence.

In a specially prepared pool at the Marine Laboratory of Florida State University, near Alligator Harbour, two Marine Studios dolphins called Albert and Betty were trained to take fish dangled in the water by a human hand. The pool had a muddy bottom that gave no echoes of its own, the water was kept turbid by the dolphins' swimming, and every sort of precaution was taken to ensure that the animals could not be using vision to locate the fish. (For instance, a screen hid the experimenters' hands and tests were done on dark, moonless nights, with no effect on the results.) The following are some of the results Dr Kellogg has described.

If the pool was perfectly quiet and a single BB shot was tossed into the water, the dolphins would respond by beaming a short burst of the creaking noise as if to examine the cause, but would at once ignore it. Half a teaspoon of water splashed into the pool would get the same response.

If a fish was put in with a splash, exploratory bursts of creaking would begin at once and one of the dolphins would make for it, creaking and wagging its head from side to side. With the dolphin Albert it was never necessary at feeding times to splash the food fish in the water because he kept sending out trial bursts of sound every ten seconds or so, as if he were searching for fish.

When thirty-six metal poles were lowered into the pool from overhead wires, eight feet apart and in a pattern that could be altered at will, the dolphins actually began to swim faster than before (in other words, when something disturbs them they don't slow down, they get a move on) and they quickly learned how to avoid touching the poles with their tail flukes, by day or night. Since the slightest sound of a collision was clearly recorded on tape, there was no guesswork in this experiment. There were a few collisions at first, then none.

Both dolphins were also able – and this to humans does

B.D.—K

seem extraordinary – to discriminate between fish of different sizes. Taking advantage of the fact that Albert and Betty had no taste for mullet and much preferred a smaller fish called spot, Dr Kellogg devised a series of tests using selected mullet that were 12 inches long and spot that were only 6 inches long. The animals learned that the fish they liked was the smaller one, and when a spot and a mullet were lowered together from behind the screen, Albert made four mistakes in his first 16 trials, but none whatever in the final 140 trials, some of which were done at night. But when only half a mullet was lowered together with a spot, which then became its equal in size, he did make mistakes. Dr Kellogg records, by the way, that these fishes were always taken from the hand 'very gently', and with the front teeth.

Lest the dolphins, in spite of every indication to the contrary, were still using some superhuman visual ability, an experiment was devised in which the use of vision would have led to error. Two fishes were suspended, but one was behind a sheet of plate glass – in other words, visible to the eye if visible at all, but not perceptible by sonar. In 202 trials made in this way, Albert made not one mistake. He never even began to approach the fish behind the sheet of glass.

There remained the possibility, however remote, that 'some chemical stimulus of taste was being employed'. As a final, almost superfluous check, a further experiment was devised in which no food reward played any part. The pool was divided in half by a long steel net with two equal openings, one of which was obstructed by a sheet of clear Plexiglass. The dolphins were then chased from one side to the other by means of two other 'motivating nets'.

Although the Plexiglass was randomly moved from one opening to the other without their knowing, the dolphins did 50 trials each with only two errors between them.

Professor Kellogg also made careful observations of the head-wagging movements that accompanied the creaking noise. These were only made in conjunction with the noise, and only when muddy water or darkness ruled out vision. They amounted in other words to a form of 'auditory scanning', and might be compared with what a human being does when using a torch on an unfamiliar path at night.

To do all these things the dolphin obviously needs a hearing system of the most acute sensitivity, and one that is perfect in its adaptation to the medium of water. But, of course, it has inherited one that long ago went to all the trouble of becoming adapted to work in air – a far less rigid medium, where sound behaves differently in several respects. So, once again, a piece of highly developed, typically mammalian equipment has had to be readapted, with extremely interesting results, as usual; and with, once again, a paradoxical victory over the fishes, whose hearing system cannot compare for versatility and usefulness with the one that left the sea and returned to it. To describe these changes means going into some complicated details of acoustics and anatomy, but I am going to make the attempt here, all the same, for the sake of the completeness of our story. Having described the remarkable things a dolphin can do with its hearing, I can hardly pass over the equipment it has evolved for doing them.

The main problem to be overcome when the land animals first left the sea was the big disparity (or, in the language of acoustical engineers, 'mismatch') that exists between the sound-conducting properties of air and animal tissue. Between *water* and animal tissue they are the same, so that in the sea there was no mismatch for the early vertebrates; but as the air-breathing animals evolved they had to face the fact that when an airborne sound is to enter part of an animal, 99·9 per cent of it is lost by reflection; only a thousandth part of it succeeds in crossing from one medium to the other. So the mammals developed three hearing aids: the external ear, or pinna, which helps to collect sound waves and direct them in; the eardrum itself, a thin, translucent disc which makes the most of the little energy it receives; and, in the bones of the middle ear, an arrangement of tiny levers that amplify the vibrations while conveying them from the eardrum to the cochlea, where eventually they reach filaments of the auditory nerve and become sensation.

The cetaceans faced this problem in reverse. When they returned to the sea the mismatch no longer existed, and the tissue and bone of their ears now had the same acoustic properties as the surrounding medium. But elimination of mismatch was not the only change. Sound waves in water *behave* differently from those in air, quite apart from what happens at the barrier between. They travel four times faster, for one thing, and with much less absorption (which means they travel farther). Moreover – and this is what affects the cetaceans particularly, as even Aristotle realised in a way – there is a tremendous difference, as between the two media, in the displacement amplitude and the pressure amplitude of a given sound. Sound waves in water have only one sixtieth of the displacement amplitude of the same sound waves in air, but sixty *times* the pressure amplitude. That is, an arriving sound in water will cause an eardrum to move only one sixtieth of the distance, but with sixty times the force, compared with the same sound wave in air. It is essential, however, that the vibrations presented to the cetacean cochlea should be much the same as they are in land mammals, for it is not possible for the sensory organ itself to be radically altered. So the changes in these vibrations must be made mechanically, before they reach the cochlea.

Again, the dolphin obviously cannot have an air tube leading in from the outside to its eardrum, or any connection between the water and the air cavities within that permit free movement of the moving parts. Instead, it must have a kind of water tube – actually, an almost closed-up tube, like the plastic coating of a fine wire – made of good sound-conducting material and beginning with two pinholes on either side of the head, as I mentioned earlier.

Lastly, the dolphin must not hear sounds by bone conduction, as we do under water. If it did so, it would have no directional sense whatever for underwater sound. To retain binaural hearing, therefore, the whole of its hearing system – the pinhole tubes and the middle and inner ear on either side – must somehow be insulated for sound from the surrounding flesh and bone.

All these problems have been overcome by the whales and dolphins; and by what means, we have recently been shown through some brilliant work done at the British Museum by F. C. Fraser and P. E. Purves. Their researches, and some of the related acoustical problems, were the subject of a discussion meeting of the Royal Society, held in 1959 and reported in the Society's *Proceedings* in 1960. What I have already said and what follows is

based on the papers delivered at that meeting by P. Vigoureux and F. W. Reysenbach de Haan, and by Fraser and
Purves, whose dissections and acoustic tests of the auditory
systems of various whales and dolphins have now revealed
the secrets that eluded Pliny when he wrote that dolphins
are 'obviously able to hear' but that 'precisely how they
do it is a riddle'.

Beginning, then, at the exterior, we have first of all the
two little pinholes that escaped the notice even of Aristotle
(who said that dolphins have 'no organ of hearing discernible'). They are only about half a millimetre in diameter
and lie behind and slightly lower than the eyes. The
sound that strikes these tiny points is the *only* sound that
can reach the dolphin's cochlea, for the whole of the
middle and inner ear has been insulated from the rest of
the body by foam-filled sinuses and air sacs. These, of
course, exploit the principle of mismatch between air and
fluid: the foam consists of millions of tiny bubbles, and
there is a 99·9 per cent loss of intensity every time a sound
wave tries to enter or leave the wall of a bubble. The
blubber, too, is a poor conducting medium for sound; so
the pinhole tube, which acoustic probes have shown to be
a good conductor, is the only way for sound to reach the
middle ear.

In *Tursiops* this tube goes straight into the eardrum.*
'I have taken a small piece of stiff wire,' W. N. Kellogg
writes in answer to a question, 'about one sixteenth of an
inch in diameter, and pushed it directly down the meatus
without its bending. After going an inch or two it strikes

* In some other odontocetes it makes an S-bend as it passes through
the blubber, thereby increasing its length significantly (like putting
the receptors on antennae) and perhaps assisting the binaural effect.

the bone of the bulla, and you can tap the bulla with it and hear the sound of the hollow bone.'

Inside, about three-quarters of an inch in from the surface, the tube ends at the dolphin's 'eardrum'. But this is no longer a drum as it is in the land mammals. In the human ear the eardrum resembles an open umbrella, about a third of an inch in diameter, with its concave surface facing outward and its spike (together with a rib or two) attached to the first of the bony levers of the ear – the one known as the malleus, or hammer. In the cetacean ear this umbrella has been nearly closed, and has become a ligament rather than a membrane. Its point is still attached to the handle of the hammer, but at quite a different angle. The hammer itself and the next bone (called the anvil) and, finally, the little stirrup bone, which vibrates in the oval window of the cochlea, all are modified and held in such a way as to alter the vibrations and make them similar to those that enter the cochlea of a land mammal. It is partly a matter of leverages (lengths and angles), and partly of the relative areas of the eardrum (or ligament) and stirrup bone. A study of the leverages by Fraser and Purves, and some ingenious acoustic tests they made with electronic gear, have shown that the bones of the middle ear make precisely the corrections that are theoretically required.

Thus, with bone conduction eliminated, and the pressure and displacement amplitudes corrected, that 'loud and alarming resonance' which Aristotle mentions has been taken care of, like so many of the dolphin's underwater problems; there are other modifications as well, of a kind too complex for description here, arising from other special requirements of underwater hearing. And to

conclude, the importance of all this to the dolphin is reflected in the structure of the cerebral cortex, where the area
known to be used for acoustic reception is tremendously
enlarged – and especially is this so in *Tursiops* – so that, in
the last analysis, the dolphin is provided, like the bat, with
a pair of ears seemingly able to do everything which in
other animals eyes can do.

There is one question not discussed in the *Proceedings* of
the Royal Society's discussion meeting, for which it would
be interesting to have the answer.

It concerns the wide range of sounds, high and low,
which in *Tursiops* seem to be associated with echo-location.
Underwater sounds that travel farthest are those of the
lowest frequency and longest wave-length; they spread in
all directions and are absorbed the least. Conversely, those
of the highest frequency and shortest wave-length do not
penetrate so far, and in them the bundle-of-ray effect is
greater. In other words, the farther away a fish may be,
the lower the frequency a dolphin would have to use to
locate it, and the nearer and smaller it is the higher the
frequency he would require to inspect it. Does this mean,
then, that the Bottlenosed Dolphin's comparatively wide
spectrum of sounds, from the low-pitched and audible
'rusty hinge' to the very high squeaks beyond our range,
has a functional significance? Should there really be two
terms – 'echo-location' to describe what is done from a
distance with the lower sounds, and 'echo-inspection' for
what is done at close range with the highest?

Clearly, dolphin sonar is an instrument of such perfection that human skin-divers can only regard it with wonder,
and considerable envy. It is comforting, all the same, for
humans to be able to find some flaw in the perfections of

the animal world, and the fact is that dolphins, no less than humans, must always look where they are going in the sea, or they may bump into things. Even dolphin sonar can fail – if it isn't used.

This was demonstrated, with sorry results for a compatriot of mine (and perhaps for the dolphin too), at a place called Whangamata, on the Bay of Plenty, New Zealand, in the summer of 1960. A dolphin that was in a hurry for social reasons crashed into the bottom of a sixteen-foot plywood runabout and put a hole in it either with its dorsal fin or with its snout. Five people had to swim to shore, and the owner, Mike Breed, lost his boat and engine – and no doubt any fondness for dolphins he may previously have had. Here is what happened, in Mr Breed's own words:*

'The incident occurred about half a mile from Clark Island. This Island is situated in the harbour mouth. I and my four companions had been out for a cruise past the Island when we spotted a school of about twenty dolphin; we turned toward them and they just kept swimming in front of the boat . . . After following and watching the school we decided to return. Having travelled about 500 yards I spotted something ahead; I turned toward it but it had disappeared. A few moments later I spotted this dolphin just ahead and slightly to the right of the boat. I was travelling at about 15 m.p.h. I did not slow down, the dolphin dived in front of the boat and a few moments later there was a bang and the boat lurched slightly. I looked over the side just in time to see the dolphin dive down deep. This was the last I saw of it. The dolphin was on its own, and I think it was trying to catch up with

* From a letter to the author.

the school. The boat, being of plywood construction, was
holed beneath the floor on the right-hand side. The hole
was at a guess about twelve inches long by about four
inches wide. The boat sank almost immediately . . .'

So our friends the dolphins – allowing for the occasional
blunder of this painful kind – have been doing for some
millions of years what our own submarines and modern
fishing trawlers have only begun to do in recent times.
And I have no doubt that Simo, the dolphin of the Lucrine
Lake, and the dolphin at Poroselene, and any others that
came when called were all using the same faculty as the
old bull dolphin at Woods Hole, with his one blind eye,
and Albert and Betty in Florida.

As for the dolphin that saved Arion, I think it no longer
safe to ridicule the suggestion that he came to the spot because he had heard that 'high-pitched song', the Orthian.

The Ancients vindicated

Now that we know so much about the dolphin, it is
time to turn back to each of the classical authors, as I
promised, and consider how near to the mark they came –
remembering always that the Greeks and Romans were
never able to keep a dolphin in a tank with glass windows
in the sides, or freeze its movements in a photograph, or
record the sounds it made, or dissect its nervous system,

and that they also lacked our knowledge of the cetaceans' ancestral history.

I think it can be said that Aristotle and Pliny – and Oppian too, in his different fashion – were guilty of very few serious mistakes and that, whether by science or intuition, they came closer to a true understanding of the dolphin's nature than many an authority of later times who thought his knowledge superior to theirs.*

Aristotle, to begin with, was clear about nearly all the main points that distinguish the dolphin from the fishes as a mammal. It is true that the fact of warm-bloodedness escaped him (since the meaning of warm blood was not understood in his time), and that he does not appear to have noticed the important distinction of the horizontal tail. Also, he frequently speaks of the dolphins as fishes ($\iota\chi\theta\acute{\nu}\epsilon\varsigma$), but then, he was really using this word as laymen and mariners do today, in the sense of 'sea creatures', and was not confusing them. On the contrary, he specifically classed the whales, dolphins, and porpoises together as $\kappa\acute{\eta}\tau\eta$ (or cetaceans as we now say), and for about two thousand years he was alone in this. He added, incidentally, 'Many people are of opinion that the porpoise is a variety of the dolphin'.

* For example, the Reverend W. Bingley, A.M., F.L.S., 'and late of Peterhouse, Cambridge', whose *Animal Biography or Authentic Anecdotes of the Lives, Manner and Economy of the Animal Creation, Arranged According to the System of Linnaeus* was a standard work of the early nineteenth century. 'The Dolphin was in great repute among the ancients', he wrote, 'and both philosophers and historians seem to have contended who should relate the greatest absurdities concerning it. . . . How these absurd tales originated it is impossible even to conjecture; for the Dolphins certainly exhibit no marks of particular attachment to mankind. If they attend on vessels navigating the ocean it is in expectation of plunder, and not of rendering assistance in cases of distress.'

Unfortunately one piece of wrong information took Aristotle off the scent at a crucial moment in his thinking. He was under the impression that in addition to breathing air the dolphin 'takes in water and discharges it by his blowhole', and this cut across one of his main classifications; for he had decided to class all animals that breathe air as terrestrial and all that 'take in water' as aquatic, and the dolphins, he thought, did both. Therefore, he said, 'one can hardly allow that such an animal is terrestrial and terrestrial only, or aquatic and aquatic only. . . . For the fact is that the dolphin performs both these processes: he takes in water and discharges it by his blow-hole, and he also inhales air into his lungs . . .' He had found a right conclusion for the wrong reason.

Most of his information, of course, was such as could be got from above the surface of the sea by fishermen and sailors through examining the occasional captured or stranded specimen, or by observing a live one caught in a net (or perhaps a captive animal like the dolphin in the Lucrine Lake).* If he had not dissected a dolphin himself, he had got his anatomical facts from people who knew what to look for. A good example is his description of the female's mammae: 'And this creature is not provided, like quadrupeds, with visible teats, but has two vents, one on each flank, from which the milk flows; and its young have to follow after it to get suckled, and this phenomenon has been actually witnessed'.

He knew that if a dolphin was trapped under water in a net it would suffocate for lack of air, but that on the other hand it 'can also live for a considerable time out of the water'.

---

* It is thought that he made his marine researches when he was living near Lesbos (the home of Arion) about 347 B.C.

He did not, of course, understand the importance of the dolphin's auditory sense, though he knew that it was present. He may be forgiven for not having discovered the tiny earhole; and, in all the circumstances, he should lose no marks for having said that while the dolphin 'has no visible organ for smell, it has the sense of smell remarkably keen'.

He reported that a dolphin when taken out of the water 'gives a squeak and moans in the air', and he distinguished these noises from the grunts of gurnet and other fishes: 'For this creature has a voice, for it is furnished with a lung and a windpipe; but its tongue is not loose,* nor has it lips, so as to give utterance to an articulate sound'.

In one important passage he has been slightly mistranslated by Sir D'Arcy Thompson. 'The dolphin, the whale, and all the rest of the Cetacea', says Thompson's version, '. . . are viviparous. That is to say, no one of all these fishes is ever seen to be supplied with eggs, but directly with an embryo *from whose differentiation comes the fish*, just as in the case of mankind and the viviparous quadrupeds'. The phrase I have quoted in italics would be better translated as 'from whose development comes the animal'.†

Aristotle described how a dolphin sleeps, presumably relying on reported observations in the wild. He was not far wrong: 'The dolphin and the whale, and all such as are furnished with a blow-hole, sleep with the blow-hole over the surface of the water, and breathe through the blow-hole while they keep up a quiet flapping of their fins; indeed, some mariners assure us that they have actually

* In fact it is.

† οὐδὲν γὰρ τούτων φαίνεται ἔχον ᾠά, ἀλλ᾽ εὐθέως κύημα᾽ ἐξ οὗ διαρθρουμένου γίγνεται τὸ ζῷον, καθαπερ ἄνθρωπος καὶ τῶν τετραπόδων τά ζῳοτόκα.

heard the dolphin snoring'. If we merely read 'tail' instead of 'fins', the statement is nearly correct, and it is scarcely spoiled by the delightful addition about snoring – which, you will notice, is carefully attributed to 'some mariners'.

His description of dolphin mating is accurate, and it speaks highly for his judgment that he accepted without scepticism the statement that two dolphins had been seen supporting 'a little dead dolphin when it was sinking'. This is another of Aristotle's statements that has been dismissed in the past as a pleasant invention. As recently as 1956 Ivan T. Sanderson in his *Follow the Whale* called it 'almost certainly' untrue. It is very far from being untrue. Not only have the Marineland dolphins exhibited this behaviour in captivity but it has been observed in the wild as well.*

It is to his credit also that he treated the phenomenon of stranding as a mystery of unknown cause. It still is. And a final point that I have already mentioned, his report of fishermen's experiments to ascertain the dolphin's life span stood alone, the only report of such experiments, until the present century.

Altogether, Aristotle made something like forty factual statements about dolphins, only three of which are nonsense – and two of these occur in a passage which, it is pleasing to find, two scholarly editors have stigmatised. The text from which the *History of Animals* has been edited in modern times contains this passage (the errors are here placed in italics): 'As a general rule the larger fishes catch the smaller ones in their mouths whilst swimming straight after them in the ordinary position; but the selachians,†

* Three field observations were discussed by J. C. Moore in the *Journal of Mammalogy*, August 1955, page 466.
† The sharks.

the dolphin, and all the cetacea must first *turn over on their backs* as their *mouths are placed down below*; this allows a fair chance of escape to the smaller fishes, and, indeed, if it were not so, there would be very few of the little fishes left, for the speed and voracity of the dolphin is something marvellous.'

It seems to me very likely that Aristotle did at some time dissect a dolphin for himself, and *un*likely that he wrote that passage as it stands. The reference to the dolphins and the cetaceans, it is thought by the editors Aubert and Wimmer, was possibly added by another hand during one of the numerous copyings of the text which alone have preserved it for us. And it may not be inappropriate to mention that the reference to the placing of the mouth is, of course, perfectly true of the dolphins' mighty relative, the sperm whale, with which the ancients were acquainted.

Historia Animalium's one other piece of nonsense about dolphins is the statement that mothers 'take their young, when small, inside them' – meaning, apparently (or at any rate in Oppian's interpretation), inside their mouths. Since the infant dolphin is fully one third of its mother's length at birth, the statement can be confidently called absurd; yet even here a plausible explanation may be found. In the first place, there are certain fishes (though perhaps not in the Mediterranean) that protect their young in this way; and if this is irrelevant, the fact remains that Greek fishermen may well have seen baby dolphins nuzzling round their mother's head – as it is now established they do in their first few weeks of life – and momentarily disappearing behind or below her in the sea. If the fish example was known to them, they might be forgiven for explaining the phenomenon in this odd way.*

* But Mrs Josephine Young Case offers a woman's explanation

There is one further statement of Aristotle's which I decline to regard as nonsense, although it is undoubtedly inexact: namely, his assertion that dolphins when short of breath will 'spring right over a ship's mast, if a ship be in the vicinity'.

This again has been treated as rank absurdity in the past, and Ivan Sanderson has written, in the book already quoted: 'They are swift and leap far out of the waves, but never over the masts of even the most paltry ships'. But who is to contradict the following observation made in New Zealand waters by a modern lone voyager, Conor O Brien, in his book *Across Three Oceans*?

'It happened this way. When I was going up from Auckland to Tonga I fell in with a school of porpoises, crossing my course at right angles. It was a pretty sight to see a score or so of them breaking out from the face of a wave simultaneously quite close aboard; it was amusing to see their antics and their struggles to dive again when they found the ship was in their way. After about half an hour they were coming thicker, they were, so to say, crowding each other at their fences, and some of them coming with an unpleasant whack into the vessel's side (for porpoises are not designed for end-on collisions like sperm whales). Lastly one of them, finding himself in a tight corner, jumped over my jib-boom. Now if any reader has the curiosity to consider my rigging plan he will see that in order to clear the boom and the bobstay and the backropes

---

that is far simpler. 'I wonder', she writes, 'if Aristotle did not mean into the body rather than into the mouth. If some fisherman had seen a half-accomplished birth [see Plate 12], he would not have realised it was a birth perhaps, because of the tail-first presentation, and thought the baby was being protected.'

and the footropes and the two jib downhauls and the flying-jib sheets, an exceptionally agile porpoise was required. When I add that all this apparatus was alternately sweeping the troughs of the seas and scraping shreds off the clouds while the ship rolled along at eight knots, not one porpoise in a hundred would take the jump. And as the ship was rolling between upright and thirty-five degrees to leeward (for there was a big beam sea) and the weather backrope was at times higher than the foot of the jib, I felt sure that the next porpoise that tried such tricks would go through that ancient and rotten sail. And as all gregarious animals tend to follow their leader, more of them would go through my newer but almost equally rotten mainsail; so I put up my helm and ran away before them, and if they tried any more high jumps they would only land in the chartroom or the galley (but I did not know then how good eating they were).'

From the sail plan given in Mr O Brien's book it would appear that his jib-boom was about ten feet above still water at its central point. At Marine Studios dolphins have been trained to snatch a fish from the end of a pole sixteen feet above the water, with only a short run to gather speed. In terms of energy, the leap that Mr O Brien saw in the open sea was thus comparatively easy. One wonders how high were the 'masts' of small Greek ships, and what 'over' meant, at second hand, in Aristotle's text.

To sum up all this: there was precious little that could have been discovered about dolphins in his day that Aristotle did not know and interpret soundly. Indeed, I think that if he could have been given some hint of the principles of the Darwinian theory of evolution, this great biologist would surely have guessed where they came from and would have said, with Oppian, that they 'exchanged the land for the sea and put on the form of fishes'.

Let us turn now to Pliny again – the elder Pliny, the author of *Natural History*. This writer added, as I have said, both fact and fiction to what Aristotle wrote. But, and this may surprise some scholars who are acquainted with his work, he added considerably more of fact than fiction. Admittedly, in describing the dolphin of the Lucrine Lake he said that when the boy got on to its back it 'sheathed the prickles of its fin', as if it had a fishlike fin. There is in fact a large fish, the *Coryphaena*, or dorado, which is widely known by the name of dolphin, and has a spiny fin along the whole length of its back. It is celebrated for its changes of colour when dying, and is mentioned in a poem by Byron. But I find no evidence that it was known as a dolphin in Pliny's time.

Pliny's reputation for absurd credulities is not un-deserved: his *Natural History* is full of them. Nevertheless, he comes closer than any classical author, including Aris-totle, to touching on the dolphin's auditory sense. 'The dolphin is an animal that is not only friendly to mankind', he writes, 'but is also a lover of music, and it can be charmed by singing in harmony, but particularly by the sound of the water organ.' The water organ, a musical instrument invented by an Egyptian about three centuries before the time of Christ, was much the same as a modern organ except that water pressure was used to blow the air through the pipes. It was capable of being terribly loud, so loud that the player had to plug his ears, and it was used in the open, at gladiatorial shows. Perhaps it was also used on festive occasions near the sea. We know now that the short pipes that give the high notes would also have given out ultrasonic vibrations such as dolphins hear and are interested in. It is therefore quite possible that dolphins were attracted by curiosity to the sound of the water organ, and the observation is far from being absurd.

Pliny also gives us what is certainly the best piece of observation of the dolphin behaviour in classical times, in his account of dolphins helping the fishermen at Narbonne. The fact that Pliny was in that province for a time and therefore probably saw the thing with his own eyes no doubt explains this. His account has all the signs, as I said before, of being a faithfully reported eyewitness description.

It gives a clear impression of the *gentleness* of the dolphins, which did not move violently if men were near, keen as they may have been to seize the mullet. It contains what may be an instance of dolphins displaying an intention – where they caught and disabled some of the mullet but did not eat them then and there, 'postponing a meal till victory is won'. And when the dolphins did get inside the fishermen's nets, they glided out again 'so gradually as not to open ways of escape; none of them try to get away by leaping out of the water, which otherwise they are very fond of doing, *unless the nets are put below them*' (italics mine). You will notice a remarkable similarity here to what was observed off the coast of Florida some nineteen centuries later and reported by A. F. McBride.* Were the waters murky in all that flurry of Gauls, nets, mullets and dolphins, and were the dolphins detecting the nets by echolocation?

I shall be dealing in more detail shortly with this question of dolphins helping human fishermen, for it has been going on for many centuries in widely scattered parts of

* See page 124.

the world and the subject deserves a chapter to itself. But let us finish re-examining the Greek and Roman authors.

The younger Pliny's account of the dolphin at Hippo has not been exempt from scepticism, and some writers have seen it as nothing more than an ornate version of the widespread boy-and-dolphin fable; but no one who saw what happened at Opononi in 1956 would make that mistake. In the light of all the facts now, it reads, surely, like a truthful account of something that actually occurred. There is the interesting detail of the second dolphin that would not submit to human contact; and Pliny can be given the credit for making the first known reference, even if it was inadvertent and even if he misunderstood it, to the sickness that can be caused in a dolphin by overheating due to removal from the water.*

Then there is Oppian – Oppian with his florid embroidering of a few slender facts, but with what a love for dolphins! Oppian is far from being a scientific writer, and if Aristotle's and Pliny's works had all been lost we should have almost no idea of the ancients' scientific knowledge of the dolphin, it is true. Yet, through his insight and his flights of imagination, how close to the *spirit* of his subject Oppian came.

Finally there is Plutarch; Plutarch whom I have chided for his anthropomorphism and for seeing human motives in dolphin behaviour. When Plutarch wrote of dolphins he was not writing natural history so much as indulging in

* The next reference, so far as I know, was in C. H. Townsend's paper 'The Porpoise in Captivity', an account of the keeping of some Bottlenosed Dolphins in a pool at the New York Aquarium in 1914. It had been found in bringing the specimens from Cape Hatteras that 'they give off much heat, and if allowed to dry develop blisters which turn into festering sores'.

a discursive literary essay on a topic that gave him pleasure. The result (which is in dialogue form) contains such pleasant nonsense as this passage on the way the dolphin sleeps: 'How much cleverer, my friend, is the artifice of the dolphin, for whom it is illicit to stand still or cease from motion. For its nature is to be ever active . . . When it needs to sleep it rises to the surface of the sea and allows itself to sink deeper and deeper on its back, lulled to rest by the swinging motion of the ground swell until it touches the bottom. Thus roused, it goes whizzing up, and when it reaches the surface, again goes slack, devising for itself a kind of rest combined with motion. And they say that tunnies do the same thing for the same reason.'

Nonsense it may be; but the fact remains that in Marineland of the Pacific, California, a captive Pilot Whale (which is, after all, a large species of dolphin) has been observed sleeping with its head on the bottom and behaving in a manner not altogether unlike that described by Plutarch. A photograph of this appeared in *Life* magazine, a few years ago.

It is Plutarch moreover (and this will have to end our examination of the ancients' knowledge and insight) who points out that the dolphin is 'the only creature who loves man for his own sake'. Of the land animals, he says, some avoid man altogether, and the tame ones, such as dogs, horses, and elephants, are tame because he feeds them; whereas 'to the dolphin alone, beyond all others, nature has granted what the best philosophers seek: friendship for no advantage. Though it has no need at all of any man, yet it is a genial friend to all, and has helped many.'

III

DOLPHINS AND MEN

. . . it shall not be lawful for any person to take the fish or mammal of the species commonly known as Risso's dolphin (Grampus griseus) *in the waters of Cook Strait, or of the bays, sounds, and estuaries adjacent thereto.*

. . . it shall not be lawful for any person to take or molest any dolphin in the Hokianga Harbour . . .

REGULATIONS: *The New Zealand Gazette,* 1904 and 1956

'THOUGH IT HAS NO NEED AT ALL OF ANY man, yet it is a genial friend to all, and has helped many.' In fact there is more truth in those last four words of Plutarch's than has yet been recognised, even in the pages of this book. Dolphins and human fishermen are a subject we have not exhausted yet. So far we have heard of it only in connection with Mediterranean shores; but this collaboration has been going on in many different parts of the world, and for a very long time, and, so far as I can discover, no one has yet brought the available accounts together in one place.

There is Pliny's to begin with – no need to go back over that – and the fishing by torchlight on Euboean shores which Oppian describes so charmingly, though not with the attention to detail one could wish for.

In fact there is a rather better description of this torchlight fishing in the pages of Aelian, a bookish, deskbound author who covered much the same ground with regard to dolphins as Pliny and Oppian, but who is seldom as worthy as they of being quoted. A Roman, born about A.D. 170, Aelian wrote in Greek, and drew exclusively on Greek authors for his prose miscellany of fact and fable, *On the Characteristics of Animals*. It was his boast that he had never once been outside Italy, never been on board a ship, and knew nothing of the sea. In the following description he repeats Oppian's mistake about the purpose of the flares, so presumably they both used the same source. Yet his account, which follows, is of more interest today than Oppian's lyrical evocation of the same scene.*

'There are stories which reach us from Euboea of fisher-folk in those parts sharing their catch equally with the dolphins in those parts. And I am told that they fish in this way. The weather must be calm, and if it is, they attach to the prow of their boats some hollow braziers with fire burning in them, and one can see through them, so that while retaining the fire they do not conceal the light. They call them lanterns. Now the fish are afraid of the brightness and are dazzled by the glare, and some of them not knowing what is the purpose of the thing they see, draw near from a wish to discover what it is that frightens them. Then terror-stricken they either lie still in a mass close to some rock, quivering with fear, or are cast ashore as they are jostled along, and seem thunderstruck. Of course in that condition it is perfectly easy to harpoon them. So when the dolphins observe that the fishermen have lit their fire, they get ready to act, and *while the men row softly* the dolphins scare the fish on the outskirts and push them and prevent any escape. Accordingly the fish, pressed on all sides and in some degree surrounded, realise that there is no escaping from the men that row and the dolphins that swim; so they remain where they are and are caught in great numbers. And the dolphins approach as though demanding the profits of their common labour due to them from this store of food. And the fishermen loyally and gratefully resign to their comrades in the chase their just portion – assuming that they wish them to come again,

* In passages quoted from various authors in the following pages I have italicised certain phrases for reasons that will be obvious.

unsummoned and prompt, to their aid, for those toilers of the sea are convinced that if they omit to do this, they will make enemies of those who were once friends.'

It is recorded by Pliny that torchlight fishing with the help of dolphins was practised also at Iasos, the home of Dionysios and Hermias, thus making three separate places where the dolphin assisted human fishermen in classical times. And it is still in use in the Mediterranean today. The Greek author Nicholas Apostolides, in his book *La Pêche en Grèce*, published in Athens in 1907, describes how fishermen of the Sporades catch quantities of garfish 'in the darkest nights of the month of October' by a technique resembling that described by Aelian.

At a chosen spot, he says, the fishermen lower their sails and row, very slowly and quietly, and listen. They are waiting to hear the noise made by dolphins as they chase a school of garfish at the surface. As soon as they hear it, they light fires of resinous wood in iron grilles fixed over their bows, and the garfish then collect around their boats. Next they gently turn their boats round in the water, a dozen times or so, as if to 'show' the light to any garfish that have not yet been attracted to it. Then they row very softly to the shore, followed by the garfish that have gathered. In shallow water (but taking care not to bump the bottom, which would scare the fish away) they ship their oars, and set to work with hand nets from either side of their boats. If the garfish try to make for the open sea, says Apostolides, they merely encounter the dolphins.

There is evidently some inaccuracy (or, at any rate, misinterpretation of causes and effects) in both this modern account and Aelian's. The same sort of night fishing is done regularly today in the Bay of Naples. My friend

Andrew Packard, who has read the typescript of this book while doing research work at the Stazione Zoologica there, believes that it is not the *fishes* that are attracted by the light – or the dolphins either, for that matter. And in order that the phenomenon can be woven, as he says, 'even more correctly and interestingly into the life story of the dolphin', he has provided the following note:

'Aelian's account is plainly unreliable in certain respects. The ways of fish and fishermen in the Mediterranean have not changed much since his day, and this is what we (and I have discussed this with the senior zoologist here, Pierre Tardent, in another context) believe to be the causal sequence in the night fishing with flares that still goes on in the Bay of Naples whose lights I can see from my window as I write this. They light their flares and *wait*, holding them just above the water, or (with the electric globes) lowering them into the water. After about twenty minutes – the time of course varies – a few fish, sardines, pipefish, squids, anchovies, etc., depending on which shoals they are following, begin to collect. The men in the boat keep absolutely quiet [note Aelian's "the men row softly"] and it is a painful procedure to go out with them to watch, as you have to sit without moving a muscle for fear of knocking the side of the boat and immediately scattering the fish. More fish collect, and the bigger ones come to feed on the smaller ones. Meanwhile the two attendant boats that always accompany the one with the flare spread out a very long net between them (a special type, introduced since the war from the Netherlands), at a distance at first and then gradually closing in on the one with the flare, encircling it with the net.

'If the fish are themselves directly attracted by the

light, then why do they scatter on the slightest disturbance? It seems most unlikely that there should be a general phototropism on the part of all these different species that are caught in this way, and I think we can almost rule this out. However it wouldn't be true either to say they are terrified by the light, as Aelian suggests. They are night-feeding species that come to feed on the plankton, and it is the *plankton* – particularly the planktonic crustacea – that are attracted by the light. They do have a positive phototropism.

'At Portobello [in New Zealand] I used to put a 500-watt bulb off the end of the wharf, and the same sequence occurred: gradually more and more crustacea or swimming polychaetes until there was a cloud, and in amongst them would come pipefish, barracuda, and others, or a green-bone if you were lucky. Most exciting. They too would shoot off at the slightest disturbance, and it was quite an art to be able to get them out with a hand net. Similarly it must have been a problem, which they have now solved here with the long Dutch nets, to capture the shoals that came to the light in the days when they only had short nets, and it may well be that they did so by rowing quietly inshore – lights, plankton, sardines, and all.

'Now the dolphins appear to come in as follows: Yesterday I asked one of our older fishermen, Sabato Milo, whether the commercial fishermen ever saw dolphins in the Bay. And without any prompting he answered: "Certainly. But there are two kinds of dolphin, the ones that help the fishermen (*Delphinus delphis*) and the ones which don't, which we call *felone* (= *Tursiops?*). They will attack the fish actually in the nets." He says that if they see dolphins, especially towards September, they will follow them until they see the fish jumping out of the water, as the dolphins drive the fish up from below. In other words, they use the dolphins to locate a shoal which they could not otherwise see. He says they have no way of calling them and do not co-operate with them to the extent of feeding them. As for Aelian's account, it is possible that dolphins do stand off from the boats with lights and keep their distance as they approach the shores, eventually perhaps scaring the fish back into the shallows; but if so, I think it is more likely to be because they themselves are scared of the lights than out of co-operation. I am sure it would have been mentioned if the dolphins had been reported coming close in to the lights themselves.'

Although there is no mention of any reward being given to the helpful dolphins either in the Sporades or the Bay of Naples, all these Mediterranean accounts have one other thing in common: neither Pliny, Oppian, Aelian, Apostolides, nor Sabato Milo expresses incredulity about the dolphins' behaviour, nor anticipates it in the reader. It is clear that in those waters, where the dolphin has for so long been understood, its useful habits are taken for granted.

But now we move to the opposite side of the world and find a different state of affairs, at least among white men. At Moreton Bay on the Pacific Coast of Queensland until about a hundred years ago, Australian aborigines were catching mullet with the help of dolphins. This happened at a particular spot in the bay and nowhere else, and the name of the spot, it is pleasing to record, was Amity Point.

The aborigines seem to have understood the animals, and knew how to call them, and even had names for particular dolphins. They also (unlike certain neighbours of theirs in Polynesia) forbade the killing of them, and believed that dreadful consequences would follow if a man were to kill a dolphin. There are several accounts of what used to happen at Amity Point, and it is evident that the white men who set them down did not expect to be believed. Because of this general scepticism – and evidently in ignorance of the Mediterranean precedents – the director of the Queensland Museum, Heber Longman, collected all the references together in 1926 in an article, 'New Records of Cetacea', which was published in the *Memoirs* of the Museum. Here is the most complete of these accounts:*

'Between the two islands which form the south part of Moreton Bay is a passage known as South Passage, formerly used for ships entering the Bay, but now given up. Near the deserted pilot station at Amity Point, some of the natives may constantly be found during the warmer months of the year fishing for "mullet", a very fine fish about the size of a mackerel. In this pursuit they are assisted in a most wonderful manner by the porpoises. It seems that from time immemorial a sort of understanding has existed between the blacks and the porpoises for their mutual advantage, and the former pretend to know all the porpoises about the spot, and even have names for them.

'The beach here consists of shelving sand, and near the shore are small hillocks of sand, on which the blacks sit, watching for the appearance of a shoal of mullet. Their nets, which are used by hand, and are stretched on a

---

* Written by Mr Fairholme, in the *Proceedings* of the [Queensland?] Zoological Society for 1856. Heber Longman explains that the animals are invariably referred to as 'porpoises' in Queensland, but that the species concerned is probably *Tursiops catalania*, a local relative of the Atlantic Bottlenosed Dolphin.

frame about four feet wide, lie ready on the beach. On seeing a shoal, several of the men run down, and with their
spears make a *peculial splashing in the water*. The porpoises
being outside the shoal, numbers of the fish are secured before they can break away. In the scene of apparent confusion
that takes place, the blacks and porpoises are seen splashing about close to each other. So fearless are the latter that
strangers, who have expressed doubts as to their tameness,
have often been shown that they will take a fish from the
end of a spear, when held to them.

'For my part I cannot doubt that the understanding is
real, and that the natives know these porpoises, and that
strange porpoises would not show so little fear of the
natives. The oldest men of the tribe say that the same
kind of fishing has always been carried on as long as they
can remember. Porpoises abound in the bay, but in no
other part do the natives fish with their assistance.'

Mr Longman cites seven other published references,
which between them give a few extra details. In Volume 8
of the *Proceedings of the Royal Society of Queensland*, for example, George Watkins stated: 'The co-operative principle was so well understood between these fellow-
adventurers, that an unsuccessful porpoise would swim
backwards and forwards on the beach, until a friend from
the shore waded out with a fish for him on the end of a
spear.' In *Tom Petrie's Reminiscences* (published at Brisbane
in 1904 but dating from 1837) it is recorded that one old
dolphin was well known and spoken of fondly by the
aborigines as the 'big fellow of the tribe of porpoises', and
Petrie says that he himself saw this dolphin take a fish
from the end of a spear. Another eye-witness of later times,
Thomas Welsby, in a book called *Schnappering*, published

at Brisbane in 1905, described how the aborigines called the dolphin in:

'I remember witnessing a great scene of fun and excite-men on the haul right in front of the reserve at Amity Point. A large school of mullet were coming in along the shore, but were too far out in the deep water for the blacks, when a number of porpoises were observed rolling about five hundred yards away, and sunning themselves, in complete unconsciousness of the feast so near them. One black fellow went down to the beach with a spear, which he prodded into the sand several times, and then *struck the water with it at full length and flat along it or horizontally*. Instantly the porpoises answered the signal by dashing in, and, of course, driving the poor mullet before them, when there was a rush of about twenty natives into them with their nets, and for the next few minutes nothing was to be seen but a confused mass of fish, porpoises, and blacks, all mixed up together, out of which the blacks emerged with their nets as full as they could hold, and left the balance of the school to be worried by the curious allies.'

From Queensland we now make a rather surprising leap across the Pacific, passing my country and Polynesia and flying over the Andes, and coming to rest again at a little village in the Mato Grosso, beside a tributary of the Amazon called the Tapajós, the name of the village being São Luiz and the time that of World War II.

Here we make the acquaintance of a new variety of dolphin, the species *Inia geoffrensis*, a primitive, pink-bellied river dolphin known locally by its native name *bouto* which also helps human beings in fishing.

Since I have done no more than mention the river dolphins up to now, this is the place for a little about them.

B.D.—M

They are not classified as Delphinidae, like *Delphinus* and *Tursiops*, but belong to the separate family known as the Platanistidae, and they differ considerably from the ocean dolphins in appearance. The reason is partly their different habitat and partly that they are a long way behind the Delphinidae in evolutionary development; in fact the genus *Inia* was described by F. E. Beddard in his *A Book of Whales* (the first and for a long time the only full account of the cetacean Order, published in 1900) as the nearest thing we know to 'the basal odontocete'. Whether this means that dolphins 'began' in rivers rather than in the sea, no one could fairly say; our knowledge is not complete enough for that. But the fact is that we have to turn to the river dolphins of the Amazon and Ganges and other large rivers to find a living creature that gives appearance of being 'on the way' to the modern perfection of the dolphin form. So we might perhaps regard them as a mammal that has not entirely left the 'forest' of which I spoke earlier, nor yet become completely adapted to that other three-dimensional element, the ocean.

The river dolphins are altogether cruder in design than the ocean dolphins. Some of them have a lumpish head, with a perceptible and mobile neck (as if the 'pushing back' and the streamlining were still in process), and the dorsal fin amounts to little more in profile than the front sight of a rifle (as if the 'pinching up' had only just begun). The outline of their tail flukes, too, would suggest imperfection to an aircraft designer, and most of them have long, oddly shaped beaks, a little suggestive of the crocodile, and much of the detail of their bone structure also marks them as primitive dolphins. The dolphins of the Ganges, locally known as *susu* (an imitation of their breathing sound) have feeble, lensless eyes, being described in some accounts as almost blind, and their feeding habit is to probe about in the mud on the river bottom. The *susu* was actually known to Pliny, by the name of *platanista*; its scientific name today is *Platanista gangetica*, and all the fresh-water dolphins are known as Platanistidae. An unusual character of the *susu* is the shape of its flippers, which are scalloped, with the five mammalian 'fingers' still discernible, as in the embryos of the more advanced species. The same is true of the *bouto* of the Amazon. The *bouto*, moreover, has not dispensed with all its hair, having a number of short vibrissae on its beak even when fully grown. Nor can it stay under water very long; it surfaces to blow at much shorter intervals than other species do. One thing can be stated definitely about the *bouto*'s distant past: fossil remains have revealed that the family it belongs to was once distributed widely throughout the oceans. Its only surviving close relative today is the White Flag Dolphin of Tungting Lake in China. All this information would suggest that the river dolphins are dolphins that have been driven or kept from the oceans by the competition of more advanced and more efficient species.

These animals are therefore very interesting, and especially so if we read an observation of the Amazon variety reported in Ivan Sanderson's *Follow the Whale*. Sanderson describes seeing a number of *bouto* in a strange and mysterious way – literally in the water and in the forest at one and the same time. The Amazon was in high flood, and his canoe was in the midst of the forest, some distance from the river itself, when a curious sighing and puffing sound drew attention to the odd pink forms lolloping through the trees with their modified mammalian gallop, as if some trick of time had brought them out of the Miocene epoch before his eyes.

But now to our *bouto* in the Tapajós River which collaborates with a human fisherman. For its description we have to thank F. Bruce Lamb, an American expert in tropical forestry who was working for the rubber-development programme in Brazil during World War II, and subsequently described what he had seen in the Tapajós in an article published in *Natural History* magazine for May 1954. It is evident that Lamb had not heard of the ways of the dolphins at Narbonne, Euboea, the Sporades, or Moreton Bay. He many times saw *bouto* playing round his launch, and watched their acrobatic antics with amazement. He learned the various local stories about the animal: how it was said by some to 'spoil the fishing'; how sometimes a lone canoeist would lose his paddle if a prankish *bouto* came up underneath and ran off with the paddle between its teeth; how *bouto* were said to have saved the lives of people whose boats had capsized by pushing them ashore; and how the dolphin denoted safety in the water, in so far as the dreaded flesh-eating *piranha* would never appear when one was near, since they would themselves be eaten. And he saw with his own eyes the uncanny disappearance of a school of *bouto*, 'as if by signal', when a mechanic on his launch tried to sneak a rifle on deck unseen to get a shot at them.

He also saw with his own eyes how an individual *bouto* assisted the fishing expedition of Rymundo Mucuim, a local mechanic and jack-of-all-trades at the village of São Luiz, below the first rapids on the Tapajós. One evening Dr Lamb went fishing with Rymundo. They paddled downriver in the tropical dusk, away from the village and the noise of the rapids to Rymundo's accustomed fishing ground. While treefrogs chirruped in the forest and the plaintive whistling of the tree sloth or the occasional watery grunt of a bull alligator gave tropical atmosphere to the night, Rymundo busied himself in the bow with his carbide lamp and harpoons, and a companion paddled the canoe. Soon Lamb was puzzled by the paddler, who started *'tapping on the side of the canoe with his paddle between strokes and whistling a peculiar call'*. Rymundo explained this by casually remarking that they were calling their *bouto*.

'This struck me as the purest nonsense,' writes Lamb, 'especially after the tales I had heard about porpoises spoiling the fishing. However, Rymundo assured me that he had a certain porpoise trained to come when he called and to help him fish. After two years in the Amazon jungles I had learned to keep an open mind towards the unbelievable, so I sat silently waiting.'

As they approached the accustomed fishing grounds near the river bank, Rymundo lit his carbide lamp and selected a harpoon. Almost immediately, about fifty feet from the canoe, a *bouto* surfaced to blow. 'Now we're all set,' said Rymundo. 'Everybody's here and ready to go.' One large brown fish was speared, in shallow water near the shore, and the canoe went on. 'As we progressed, the fish *scattered ahead of us and went for deep water, but there they encountered our friend the porpoise*, who was also fishing, and so they came rushing back to the shallows. Several times they sped back so fast they ended up flopping on the beach.'

Then they saw something that had nothing whatever to do with dolphins, though Oppian might have seen some connection, and possibly Aristotle too. Rymundo drew

Lamb's attention to a large fish, a *tucunare*, with its young, and they saw the fingerlings being gathered for protection into the parent's mouth – entering within her teeth and lingering in the maternal mouth, as Oppian wrote of the dolphins. Sparing the adult to conserve the young, Rymundo lowered his harpoon and they paddled on downstream. Many more fish were caught, but at length Rymundo decided to cross the river to another area. The crossing took about a quarter of an hour, and meanwhile the *bouto* (whose presence was always evident from its frequent surfacing and blowing) disappeared. It was explained to Lamb that the pace of the paddled canoe was too slow for the dolphin, and it would be 'waiting when we arrived at the new fishing grounds'.

And so it was, waiting off shore again and 'giving us his full support and no doubt getting just as good a catch as we were'. As they returned to São Luiz toward midnight, the fishermen assured Lamb that this same *bouto* helped them in all their night fishing, 'scaring the fish from the deep water back to the shallows just as the fishermen scared them out to the porpoise'.

There seemed little doubt, says Dr Lamb, that Rymundo's fishing benefited by the *bouto*'s actions: 'Although some scientists may not agree that wild animals can be induced to co-operate with man in the manner indicated by this experience, I would urge them to await further checking by other careful observers. The porpoise actually accompanied us at fifty to a hundred feet for over an hour. This differed greatly from the random feeding movements I have seen porpoises engage in on other occasions.'

Dr Lamb might have been less surprised by what he saw in Brazil had he known that a similar relationship between human fishermen and river dolphins has been reported from Asia too. The animal in this case was the Irrawaddy River dolphin *Orcella fluminalis*, of which it is recorded in John Anderson's *Account of the Zoological Results of Two Expeditions to Western Yunnan* (1879) that 'the fishermen believe that the dolphin purposely draws fish to their nets, and each fishing village has its particular guardian dolphin which receives a name common to all the fellows of his school . . . Colonel Sladen has told me that suits are not infrequently brought into the native courts to recover a share in the capture of fish, in which a plaintiff's dolphin has been held to have filled the nets of a rival fisherman.'

Leaving the river dolphins and the tropics, we return to Australia, and come to what may seem the strangest of all these tales of Delphinidae and human fishermen. The place this time is Twofold Bay, New South Wales, on the south-eastern corner of Australia, and the period the first part of the present century and earlier. Our authority for the affair is W. J. Dakin, formerly Professor of Zoology in the University of Sydney (and before that at Liverpool), who described it in his book *Whalemen Adventurers*, published in Sydney in 1934; and the 'dolphin' on this occasion is the ferocious *Orcinus orca*, or so-called Killer Whale, which assisted in the capture of Humpback Whales by men. Once again, before I can tell the story it is necessary to say a little about a species that I have so far mentioned only briefly.

'Killers' are not really whales in the usual sense of that word (though personally I am glad they are not called dolphins, either). They are the largest member of the family Delphinidae and are extremely savage, being the only cetaceans, so far as is known, that will attack and eat another cetacean or another mammal. Like most savage animals, they exhibit their character in their appearance. Their dorsal fin, five or six feet high and tapered like a racing sail, skims above the water with a menacing appearance that identifies them instantly – no other whale or dolphin has such a fin. Their black body is marked with patches of white or yellow in a pattern of cruelty rather than of grace. They have mean faces, and a throat large enough to swallow a small dolphin whole. They also devour seals (although in that case, it has been said, they have to spit the fur out afterwards), and the stomach of one twenty-four-foot Killer Whale when captured was found to contain the skeletons of fourteen seals and thirteen dolphins. That they engage in fierce combats has been deduced from the fractures found in very large bones of skeletons taken for museums. They attack their prey in packs, which has earned them the reputation of being the wolves of the sea, and they have been seen to set upon a great baleen whale many times their own size. It is their habit to seize the flippers and tail flukes and torment the whale until its tongue lolls out. Then they bite out the tongue and eat away the lips, and, having fed on the tender parts, they leave the rest.

In the Antarctic, it is said, Killers raise their heads onto the edges of ice floes in quest of seals, which slither toward them as the ice floe tilts; and in *Scott's Last Expedition* there is a vivid description by Captain Scott of a narrow escape experienced by the photographer Herbert Ponting when he tried to photograph a pack of Killer Whales which had spotted a pair of the expedition's dogs tied up on an ice floe. The Killers bumped the floe from underneath and split it into fragments. Scott speaks with awe of their 'huge, hideous heads', their small glistening eyes, and 'their terrible array of teeth – by far the largest and most terrifying in the world'.

It is evident that other men, too, who have seen the Killer Whale close at hand – including men who have recently been down in the Antarctic for the International Geophysical Year – have felt an instinctive fear of them on sight.

But now to our story of Killer Whales helping men. Twofold Bay is a deep, sheltered inlet extending about five miles from the ocean to its innermost part. It lies beside a natural route to the tropics for migrating Baleen Whales, which go there from the south to have their young; and it was also the stamping ground in the old whaling days of a famous character of New South Wales, Ben Boyd. Its inmost fold was the site of West Boyd Town and the Seahorse Inn, and on the ocean side of its southern head there still stands Ben Boyd's Tower, an imposing square stone structure of medieval appearance, which was erected as a lookout. The type of whaling used there was the ancient style called bay whaling, the first that man employed, which relies on catching such whales as are sighted from land and bringing them to a tryworks near the beach. It was begun there in 1866 by a Scotsman named Alexander Davidson, and it was carried on by Davidson's descendants, with scrupulous attention to the old traditional courtesies of the era of Moby Dick, until about thirty years ago. When Professor Dakin visited the place in 1932 to investigate the story of the Killers, the authentic atmosphere of the old whaling days could still be savoured; the tryworks stood on the beach near the windlass and the ramp, two whaling boats lay decaying in a shed, and three old-stagers, keen-eyed men of the sea, were still available to tell the story which had come to its close only two years earlier. There was other evidence as well to recall what had happened, preserved with care in the little township of Eden on the north side of the bay; but this belongs to the end of Professor Dakin's story.

Regularly in July of every year (Dakin was told by old George Davidson) the Killer Whales used to arrive off the entrance to the bay, presumably from the Antarctic. Among them were certain well-known individuals which could be recognised by the whalemen and were known by name: Old Tom, for example, whose dorsal fin had a curious small projection on its forward edge, in outline not unlike a rose thorn; Hookey, whose fin had a noticeable bend in it; and also Humpy and Stranger. Of these, and what they were alleged to have done, Dr Dakin had already heard a little in Sydney. He had decided to visit the place and question the men themselves.

According to James Morgan, who used to go out in Davidson's boat, there were three distinct mobs of Killers in the past. One mob did sentry duty about a mile out from the heads, another went both shoreward and outward across the second mile, and a third took stations farther out. They were waiting, so the whalemen believed, for their quarry, the migrating Baleen Whales, and especially for the females, heavy with young. It is thought that their chief prey was the Little Piked Whale, but there were also migrating Humpbacks; and if any seals had established colonies on the coast, 'they did not come amiss'.

One morning at dawn in the old days, says Dakin, while the whalemen of Boyd Town or Eden were still in their beds, a gravid Humpback would come slowly past the heads. Were it not for the Killer Whales she might have passed by unnoticed, but thanks to the Killers her presence would be known, for 'there is grand excitement amongst them', and the mobs set up a noisy and unmistakable activity known to the men as 'flop-tailing'. The noise of flop-tailing made by the inshore packs would be heard from the lookout and the signal then was given to launch the boats.

'It is definitely stated and implicitly believed', according to Dakin, 'that the killer whales deliberately threw their bodies out of the water to attract the attention of the whalers on shore.' (It would be sufficient explanation, of course, to say that the function of the Killers' behaviour was to inform *each other* of the presence of their prey, and to bring the packs together; however, the private interpretation put upon it by the men does not affect the facts.)

When flop-tailing has mobilised the Killers, and informed the whalers as well, the chase is on. Let Dr Dakin describe it, with his unconscious echoes of the classical writers. 'The whale, harassed by the killers, does her best to get out to sea, whilst the aim of her foes is to prevent her gaining open water, to harry her and keep her close inshore. There is a huge advantage to the whalemen in this manœuvre. First there is very often a considerable difference between the conditions of the sea within Twofold Bay and outside it, where one lacks the shelter of the heads. Secondly, the men are saved a considerable amount of energy in rowing. A fair indication of what the killers meant to the Eden whalemen is provided by the fact that when aided by the killers they have been able to capture their quarry within one hour. Without such help, twelve hours have frequently been insufficient time.'

At last the Humpback is harpooned, the steersman and harpooner change places (according to a whaler's custom that Herman Melville would have understood), and the erratic tow toward the shore begins. It is here that the Killers performed a concerted and peculiar action:*

'Four of the killers separate from the rest, and whilst two of them station themselves underneath the head of the whale, so preventing her from sounding, the others swim side by side, from time to time throwing themselves out of the water on top of her and right across her blowhole. They are speedily thrown off again, but the action is continued, as if the killers were well aware that by so doing they hindered the breathing of the whale.'

It was during these exciting stages of the hunt that the ways of the individual Killers were most closely observed. The best-known individual was Old Tom, who had the reputation of being a 'good worker' but also a dreadful nuisance: 'He had discovered a bit of play which annoyed the whalemen extremely. It pleased him to grab the harpoon line between his teeth and hang on to it, apparently for the excitement of being dragged forcibly through the water.'

It was said he had hung on to the line for twenty and thirty minutes at a time, and Dakin felt there was no doubt of this after hearing a Mr Logan, 'an educated and highly intelligent observer', describe a tussle between Old Tom and himself, in which a boat hook was much in use and 'both man and whale were mightily annoyed'.

Finally the tiring Humpback is approached and lanced. The whalemen are covered in blood, the sea is red, and

* 'This part of their story is indeed surprising,' says Dakin, 'but the men are in agreement as to the facts; they were interviewed by me separately, at places 300 miles apart.'

blood spouts out from the blowhole of the quarry – a sign of mortal injury. In its dangerous final flurry the whale gives up and dies. The game must then be finished according to the rules, and these, says Dr Dakin, 'give the next move to the killers':

'First they press the jaws of the dead whale up and down until they manage to get the mouth open. Having succeeded, they dive in for that delicacy, the tongue, each obtaining its mouthful . . . Full of fun like a lot of boys, they dive and leap under the boat and out of the water again and again for half an hour or more.' Meanwhile the whalemen attach an anchor to the harpoon line, and drop it, and go home, leaving the quarry (but at no loss to themselves) to the Killers: 'It is their time for reward, for their share of the prey, and payment for work done. Morgan stated that the killers actually caught hold of the head, the tail-flukes, and the fins, and took the whale down. In any case, after twenty to twenty-eight hours, the whale will rise again distended by the gases of putrefaction. The killer whales interfere no more; strange to say, they seem contented with the tongue and lips which they have removed.'

Dakin had found this story unbelievable to begin with, and partly because he was under a misapprehension: 'Nowhere else in the world', he writes at the start of his chapter on the subject, 'has the killer whale, or indeed any member of the cetacean group, been known to exhibit co-operation with human beings.'

It is perhaps not surprising that a zoologist thirty years ago should have been unaware of the precedent at Narbonne, in view of Pliny's not unmerited reputation for relating the absurd; it *is* surprising that the Professor of

Zoology at Sydney had not seen the article 'New Records of Cetacea' published by the Queensland Museum six years earlier.

This is not yet the whole of the tale. Back in Sydney, and after he had started writing the chapter about it, Dakin consulted in the Mitchell Library the unpublished diary of Sir Oswald Brierly, a 'character' of the early days at Twofold Bay and an English painter who had spent some time there in the 1840s, when the great Ben Boyd was on the rampage, and later had returned to England, become respectable, and a knight. Brierly had always meant to write a book about his whaling days, and had he done so, he would no doubt have expanded the following entry in his diary (which was quite unknown to the whalemen Dakin interviewed):

'They [the Killers] attack the whales in packs and seem to enter keenly into the sport, plunging about the boat and generally preventing the whale from escaping by confusing and meeting him at every turn . . . The whalemen of Twofold Bay are very favourably disposed towards the killers and regard it as a good sign when they see a whale "hove to" by these animals because they regard it as an easy prey when assisted by their allies the killers. The natives of Twofold Bay regard the killers as incarnate spirits of their own departed ancestors and in this belief they go so far as to particularise and identify certain individual killer spirits.'

And now we come to the end of the story, and it is in the style of the old Greek tales, and might have been made expressly for Oppian or Plutarch to embellish, had they admitted the behaviour of *Orcinus* (as I can only just bring myself to do) to the canon of dolphin lore.

Old Tom was still at large in 1928, and so was Hookey, but they were the only survivors of the pack. By then the Eden whaling station was approaching its extinction. Soon afterwards the tryworks and caldrons lay open and deserted and the whaleboats were rotting away with bracken growing up over them. Hookey was last seen in 1928, and Old Tom – who had been known there for fifty years at least, according to Dr Dakin's inquiries – returned for two more years. In September of 1930 he was seen under conditions which seemed to indicate that something was wrong. Next day his corpse was discovered washed up on the beach. According to Logan and Davidson there was no doubt of his identity. No wounds were visible, and there was no one to say authoritatively from what cause he had died. 'It is characteristic of the regard in which the killers were held', says Professor Dakin, 'that no thought was taken of rendering down "Old Tom" for oil.'

Drawings and measurements were therefore made, the blubber was hacked away, the bones were removed and cleaned, and the complete skeleton was mounted in 'a suitable building in the main street of Eden', where Dakin saw it and admired the competence of the work. A great piece had been knocked out of one side of his jaw and some teeth were missing, being probably lost at the time of the same accident. The most interesting fact to a zoologist was that all the teeth, and especially the front ones, were 'worn down to rounded bosses'. From the fact that the odontocetes do not use their teeth for grinding, but only for capturing food or fighting, Dakin considered that 'the worn knobs of ivory tell their own story'. He unhesitatingly accepted Old Tom's age as being 'eighty years or more'.

Professor Dakin called the whaling at Twofold Bay 'an

amazing co-operation', and added, 'one might also call it an intelligent co-operation'. But there is no need to stretch the facts as far as that, in any of these stories; they are remarkable enough as they stand. Not at Euboea, Narbonne, or the modern Sporades, at Moreton Bay, on the Tapajós, or at Twofold Bay is there any evidence that the animals were intelligently co-operating with men in the way that men co-operate with one another. All that is happening in every case is the same phenomenon that I can see for myself quite often if I use field glasses on a bay of Wellington Harbour not far from where I am writing these words: two animals are seeking the same prey at the same place under conditions that make the presence of each an advantage to the other. On Wellington Harbour a school of *kahawai* encounter a school of sprats and chase them, and the sprats make vainly for the surface. The resulting flurry attracts a flock of terns, which are constantly on the watch for the signs of such a battle, and at once the situation known as commensalism is set up – the *kahawai* and tern are feeding at the same table. Actually in this case the thing is carried one stage further by a couple of boys I know who live nearby. When *they* see the terns wheeling and diving over a patch of disturbed water, they get out their boat and make for the spot with fishing lines, and catch as many of the *kahawai* as they want, thanking the sprats and the terns for their unwitting assistance.

However, when the collaborating animals are dolphins, and the collaboration is with man, the temptation to see intelligent motivation in what is being done must obviously be very much greater; and in my opinion the courtesies should be preserved, and all assistance given to fishermen by dolphins should be properly rewarded afterwards, as it was by the Gauls, by the ancient Greeks, by the aborigines of Moreton Bay – and by the whalemen of Twofold Bay.

Where will all this end? Within the last year or two the noted English marine biologist Sir Alister Hardy has put forward the interesting theory that not only was man a more aquatic animal in the past, but he is about to become so again, and very soon, and for the same reason as formerly. It is already recognised that the pressure on human food resources is going to force us back to the sea for more food than we at present take from there. Hardy believes that with the help of aqualungs and a kind of atomic-powered underwater scooters of neutral buoyancy we shall soon be harvesting fish from the seabeds by far more efficient methods than we use at present. He foresees (when the political difficulties have been overcome) a change from mere hunting in the sea to a sort of farming. He thinks we may soon be 'weeding' the sea bottom of the starfishes and other invertebrates that at present compete with the fishes for their food, and may be dragging large nets about the bottom with underwater scooters and hoisting them up to waiting vessels at the surface. Clearly, such methods might well be more efficient than present trawling methods are, even with the help of sonar for locating schools. But no amount of atomic fuel and skilled design and man-made sonar would ever be able to compete in such a business with the dolphin, the most superbly equipped of all animals that has ever chased fish in the sea.

Will Sir Alister Hardy's sea-farmers, I wonder, soon be using the dolphin as a sheep farmer uses his dogs at mustering time? I don't think this question is as absurd as it might appear at first. After all, there was probably some

B.D.—N

moment in prehistory when one prehistoric man said to his companion, 'No, you'd never get *dogs* to chase your animals for you.' * Whether dolphins could ever be bred and tamed to work for man would depend in the first place on their existing habits. Do they, to begin with, have a home range? Would it be according to their natures to stay around in one locality? The answer would appear to be yes. Have they a social nature? Are they accustomed to co-operating in the wild, and in particular do they have a boss to their social group, to whom they admit subservience? The answer hardly needs repeating. Do they show an existing inclination to associate with man? It would be hard to think of any wild animal that shows a stronger one.

It is perhaps already time for man to begin experimental work to see whether dolphins can be successfully domesticated, bred for their points as dogs are bred, and trained to herd fish into his nets. The chief problems would presumably be the two inducements – food and mating needs. These do not seem insuperable. Dolphins appear to have strong preferences for particular food fishes. If plentiful supplies of the preferred ones were made available (and this is a simple matter with modern refrigeration and transport) domesticated dolphins might be conditioned to a life of partial and voluntary captivity spent near compounds linked to the sea – and more easily so if captive mates were also part of the inducement to come home. It is clear that only a system of *rewards*, not punishments, would work; and this would be an interesting moral test for man. And if ever all of this should come about, that fanciful poet Oppian would be vindicated for what he

* But see Konrad Lorenz's *Man Meets Dog* for an expert discussion of this question.

wrote of the dolphin at Poroselene: 'No dog trained to the bidding of the hunter is so obedient to follow where he leads; nay, nor any servants are so obedient, when their master bids, to do his will willingly, as that friendly dolphin was to the bidding of the youth, without yokestrap or constraining bridle.'

Polynesian tales

◦   ◦   ◦   ◦

The Pacific Ocean is a long way from the Mediterranean Sea, and the Polynesians could hardly have heard the dolphin stories of the Greeks. But there were various legendary stories among them of friendly acts to man by sea-creatures, which I feel sure relate to dolphins. There are also, I am sorry to say, some parts of Polynesia where dolphins are repaid for their trusting ways with acts of appalling barbarity. To the atoll dwellers of the Gilbert Islands, for instance, who are really a gentle and kindly people, but who live on a diet mainly of coconuts and fish, the dolphin is a friend who provides a rich supply of good red meat; and his capture in schools is celebrated with emotions that Oppian would have regarded with horror.

The ritual of porpoise-calling in the Gilberts is described by Sir Arthur Grimble in his book *A Pattern of Islands*. It is not clear from his account what species of porpoise or dolphin is involved. The coast-loving *Tursiops* would not be common in those waters, but I fear the victim may be *Delphinus delphis*, who is more oceanic than *Tursiops*. It is impossible to evade the thought; but I shall do as Grimble does and call the animals of his story porpoises.

Grimble, who was for many years an administrator in the Gilberts, was a very thin man, and it was with the idea of making him fatter and more chiefly that the ritual was enacted for him on Butaritari atoll. It was common rumour in the Gilberts, he writes, that certain tribes had the power of porpoise-calling, but 'it was rather like the Indian rope trick; you never met anyone who had actually witnessed the thing'. At Kuma village, however, there lived the hereditary porpoise-callers of the High Chiefs of Butaritari and Makin-Meang. There was one, a leading expert, who could put himself into the right kind of dream on demand: 'His spirit went out of his body in such a dream; it sought out the porpoise-folk in their home under the Western horizon and invited them to a dance, with feasting, in Kuma village. If he spoke the words of the invitation aright (and very few had the secret of them) the porpoises would follow him with cries of joy to the surface.'

On a blazing hot day when the trade-wind was stilled, Grimble was paddled for six hours over the lagoon to Kuma – a big village then, with its houses stretching for half a mile or more along the lagoon's edge beneath the coconut trees. The house of the 'dreamer' – the porpoise-caller – lay near the middle of the village. As Grimble arrived this fat, friendly man came waddling down the lagoon beach to meet him. A little tactlessly, Grimble at once asked him when the porpoises might appear. The dreamer replied that he would have to go into his dream

first; and please, from now on, would Grimble be careful
to refer to them only as 'our friends from the west'. The
other name was tabu. If he said it aloud, they might not
come.

The place was dead quiet that afternoon under the palm
trees. The children had been gathered in under the
thatches, the women were absorbed in plaiting garlands of
flowers, and the men were silently polishing their cere-
monial ornaments of shell. The makings of a feast lay
ready in baskets. Clearly, everyone expected something
to come of the business.

Some time after four o'clock, 'a strangled howl burst
from the dreamer's hut', and the dreamer dashed into the
open. He stood awhile clawing at the air, says Grimble,
and 'whining on a queer high note like a puppy's'.* Then
words came out: '*Teirake! Teirake!* (Arise! Arise!) . . . Our
friends from the west. . . . Let us go down and greet them.'

A roar went up from the village, and everyone rushed
over to the other beach, on the atoll's ocean side. They
strung themselves out and splashed through the shallows,
all wearing the garlands woven that afternoon. Breast-
deep in the water, they waited. Then, in the glare of the
sun on the water, the porpoises appeared, 'gambolling
towards us at a fine clip'. Everyone was screaming hard.
When the porpoises reached the edge of the reef they
slackened speed, spread out, and started cruising back and
forth in front of the human line. Then suddenly they
vanished.

Grimble thought they had gone away. But in a moment
the dreamer pointed downwards, murmuring: 'The king

* Whether at Tainaron, Woods Hole, or Butaritari, it is always a
high-pitched note.

out of the west comes to greet me.' There, not ten yards away, was the great shape of a porpoise, 'poised like a glimmering shadow in the glass-green water. Behind it followed a whole dusky flotilla of them.'

The porpoises seemed to be hung in a trance. Their leader came close by the caller's legs. He turned to walk beside it as it idled towards the shallows. Grimble followed a foot or two behind its almost motionless tail, and a babble of quiet talk sprang up as the villagers welcomed their invited guests to the feast on shore. 'As we approached the emerald shallows, the keels of the creatures began to take the sand; they flapped gently as if asking for help. The men leaned down to throw their arms around the great barrels and ease them over the ridges. They showed no least sign of alarm. It was as if their single wish was to get to the beach.'

When the water stood only thigh deep, the men crowded round the porpoises, ten or more to each beast. Then 'Lift!' shouted the dreamer, 'and the ponderous black shapes were half dragged, half carried, unresisting, to the lip of the tide. There they settled down, those beautiful, dignified shapes, utterly at peace, while all hell broke loose around them. Men, women, and children, leaping and posturing with shrieks that tore the sky, stripped off their garlands and flung them around the still bodies, in a sudden dreadful fury of boastfulness and derision. My mind,' says Grimble, 'still shrinks from the last scene – the raving humans, the beasts so triumphantly at rest.'

The Maoris, the branch of the Polynesian people who migrated to New Zealand, came south to the home of coastal-dwelling dolphins. They also came into the latitude of Greece. We lie at the same distance from the Equator and the Pole as the Greek archipelago, and our northern waters have an almost Mediterranean climate, very suitable for *Tursiops* and *Delphinus*, and for the Dusky Dolphin, Hector's Dolphin, the White-headed Dolphin, and others that were unknown to the Greeks. The Maoris of course were great fish-eaters too. In the islands they had come from, their men and boys spent half their lives in the water, and in New Zealand they could not have failed to become well acquainted with that other intelligent mammal who was seeking the same snapper or the same mullet for his food.

The Maoris had no written language until the European came, but many of their tribal legends have been written down since then, and it is here that one would expect to find any dolphin stories. The Maori name for the dolphin was *aihe*. They distinguished him from the porpoises (for which they had at least four different names) and of course from the whale, whose name was *paraoa*. I can find no *aihe* in their tribal stories, but I am satisfied that the dolphin is there all the same, in the guise of the *taniwha*, the legendary beasts that were sometimes met on land and sometimes in the sea. It is a well-known fact that, while nearly all the land-dwelling *taniwha* were cruel, dragon-like creatures, the ocean *taniwha* were always benevolent, gentle, and helpful. They therefore were surely dolphins.

The resemblance between the dolphin-lore of the Maori and the Greeks goes further than that. There was one Maori story of a man who, for a punishment, was caused by magic to enter the body of a porpoise and remain there for ever. There was a *taniwha* that saw to the rescue of a small boy, the son of a chief, who had been thrown from a canoe to drown. There was an occasion when a whole school of *taniwha* came to the funeral of an old man. And there was a cetacean who submitted to carrying a man on his back to his destination, and then died there on the beach.

Aside from these stories, there were three ways in general in which the ocean *taniwha* assisted men. They rescued people whose canoes had been wrecked or swamped; they escorted canoes across the sea, guiding them to islands they wished to reach; and they carried people on their backs when they had no canoes. Whenever their help was needed, a Maori would call for them, using certain invocations that were kept for the purpose.

The name of the man who was turned into a porpoise for a punishment was Ruru. The story goes that many generations before the white man came to New Zealand, two men loved a girl, and Ruru, the one she rejected, threw her over a cliff. The other man then fought him, and Ruru also was flung on the rocks below. As he fell, he made the mistake of uttering a powerful curse reserved for chiefs, which killed a porpoise that happened to be in the sea below the cliff. The porpoise was washed up on the rocks; and seeing this, Ruru went for help to the *tohunga*, or tribal priest, and offered to atone for his madness. The *tohunga* was so enraged that Ruru, not being a chief, had dared to use the curse, that he ordered him into the body of the porpoise he had slain, and ruled that he must never leave that coast, and must meet every canoe that passed it, and he was to do this for all time. This legend was recalled much later, when steamships had replaced canoes along that coast.

The name of the boy who was saved from drowning by a *taniwha* was Te Whare. He was five years old, and the son of one of the chiefs of the Ngapuhi tribe, in the northern part of the North Island. The Ngapuhi had planned an expedition in their war canoes, probably to raid some other tribe, and when they set out Te Whare and his father were in the leading canoe, which was commanded by another chief, a younger man.

As it happened, there had recently been a quarrel between the younger and the older chief, and as soon as the canoe had drawn away from land the younger man said to the elder, 'We will throw you overboard.' But he changed his mind and said, 'No, we will spare you, but your son shall be thrown overboard, and will quench the fires that are surging within you and me.' The young chief's word was law in that canoe, and at a sign strong hands threw the little boy over the side. Te Whare's father watched this happen without showing any emotion. Silently, lest he give away what he was doing, he chanted certain invocations for the boy's safety. He had given his son into the care of the ocean *taniwha*, and he called on them now to come and save him.

The canoe went on. No one but the father looked behind; and he saw a *taniwha* appear, and approach the canoe. A *taniwha* in those times would make his presence known by bumping the canoe from underneath, which told the voyagers they were safe whatever the wind might do. This message was given silently to Te Whare's father.

Then the *taniwha* swam to the boy. Te Whare naturally thought it was a monster come to eat him, and was terrified, but the *taniwha* understood this, and, realising that the boy would resist any effort to hold him, he played round with him in the water until he was too exhausted to struggle any longer. He then carried him to the nearest point of land, and left him there, and disappeared. Unfortunately for Te Whare, some women from Maunga-kiekie who were gathering the shellfish known as *pipis* found him there, and took him home to their village, so that he grew up as a slave in a hostile tribe. And in manhood he became a chief among his own people once more, and married Tamaki. . . . But that is another, and a very long story.

The name of the man who rode on a cetacean's back was Kae. I say cetacean in this case because the animal Kae rode on is called a whale in the story; but I feel satisfied that it was actually a dolphin, for a reason that will appear.

Many generations ago there was a chief named Tinirau, who lived on an island called Motutapu (or Sacred Island). Tinirau had three wives, of whom the youngest, named Hinauri, was a waif from the ocean, where she had floated about for a long time until she became covered with sea-weed and barnacles. In this condition she was stranded on Motutapu, and on being found and looked after she became the wife of Tinirau. (His two older wives objected to this, and wanted to kill Hinauri; but when they came to do it, uttering their curses, she recited a powerful spell of her own, and they fell on their backs and died.)

In due course Hinauri gave birth to a son, who was named Tuhuruhuru (or Feathered Lord), and when he was old enough to be given such a present his father gave him a pet whale – perhaps because his mother had come from the sea. The whale was named Tutunui, or Big Gamboller. Now in Maori custom the son of a chief had

to have certain ceremonies performed over him in boyhood by a *tohunga*, so Tinirau sent for a particularly
skilful *tohunga* whose name was Kae. He had him brought
by canoe to Motutapu, and arranged for the usual huge
feast to follow the ceremony. While the feast was being
prepared, Tinirau decided to pay Kae the honour of a very
special dish – a piece of rashness he later regretted. He
called Tutunui to come in from the sea, where he was
gambolling about on his own, and when Tutunui had run
himself into the shallow water, Tinirau had a piece of his
fat side cut off, and roasted in an earth-oven for Kae.

Kae performed the ceremonies over Tuhuruhuru, and
then gorged himself at the feast. He particularly enjoyed
the delicious roasted flesh of Tutunui. Afterwards he said
he wanted to go home, and a good canoe was got ready,
with plenty of strong paddlers to take him. But Kae said
he objected to that canoe, and he stayed on. It was all a
trick on his part. What he wanted was to borrow Tutunui,
supposedly for the journey home, but really so that he
could steal him from Tinirau. After hedging about for a
time, Tinirau at length consented to let Kae borrow
Tutunui for the journey, and he gave him the most exact
instructions for using the animal correctly. 'When you are
getting near the shore and he begins to shake himself,' said
Tinirau, 'then be quick and jump off on the right side.'

So Kae left Motutapu on the back of Tutunui, and
before very long he reached his own shore. Tutunui began
to shake himself, but Kae would not get off; he stayed on
Tutunui's back, pronouncing magic spells, and he pressed
him down in the shallow water, and held him down, so
that his blowhole became blocked with sand and shingle.

Now it will be clear why I think Tutunui was a dolphin:

for no man, not even Kae with his magic spells, could hold down a whale. Moreover, whales do not live near one place all the year round as dolphins do; and who would choose a whale as a pet for a boy if it was always going to be away, and when the dolphin is so much readier to be tamed, and has so often chosen a boy to be his friend?

I am sorry to say that Tutunui the dolphin died when his blowhole was blocked, and Kae got his people to cut him up and cook him. And the smell of his flesh drifted over the sea to Tinirau, who came with all his warriors to the land of Kae. . . . But once again that is another story, and a long one.

The name of the man whose funeral was attended by a school of *taniwha* was Te Tahi o te Rangi. He belonged to the Ngatiawa tribe, in what is now called the Bay of Plenty, a large bay facing out to the Pacific and the Polynesian homeland, and near the thermal region of New Zealand. One year when Te Tahi was a young man there were many floods on the lands of the Ngatiawa, and all their food crops on the low ground were ruined. Te Tahi, who was known to be gifted with magic, was suspected of having caused these floods, so the people decided to maroon him on Whakaari. This island – White Island, as it is called today – lies some miles out in the Bay of Plenty, and is really a small volcano in the sea: a horrid, sulphurous place, with boiling mud-pools, vents of steam and gas, lakelets of acid, and very little growing on it apart from some stunted trees. No one can live there. Te Tahi's people intended that he should die.

The canoes paddled back to the mainland, and Te Tahi stood watching them go out of sight for a while. But then he climbed on a high rock and, using the proper incantations, he called on the ocean *taniwha* to help him. They came, and heard the facts, and one of them took Te Tahi on his back; soon it was carrying him homeward at a pace that no canoe could match. As they passed the canoes the *taniwha* asked if he should overturn them and drown the people. (This is the only case of undolphinlike behaviour in a *taniwha* that I know of.) But Te Tahi said, 'Leave them for shame to punish. Let us acquire fame by means of mercy.' So they went on, and Te Tahi was landed safely near the mouth of the Whakatane river, and returned to his home at Opuru.

When he died there in his old age, all the *taniwha* came from the sea, and carried his body away, and now Te Tahi himself is a *taniwha* whose special task it is to rescue his descendants from the sea. To this day it is said among the Ngatiawa that no one descended from Te Tahi has ever met his death by drowning. I have no way of proving that the *taniwha* that rescued Te Tahi was a dolphin; I can only feel sure that if ever a Maori was helped ashore by a sea creature, then the creature was one of our dolphin friends.

Pelorus Jack

And now from the realm of legend to the realm of fact again. The story of Pelorus Jack is no legend – although the event was connected by Maoris at the time with the tale of Ruru and the porpoise – but is something that actually happened in New Zealand in the age of cameras and newspapers and the telegraph.

That Pelorus Jack existed, no one denies. The only doubtful thing about him is his sex. It may be that he was really Pelorus Jill, and strictly speaking, perhaps, I should preserve the doubt and refer to him as 'it'. But to the many hundreds of people still living for whom a sight of Pelorus Jack was one of the excitements of their youth – and especially to the several dozen who have given me their recollections for this book – that would be unthinkable.

He was not one of our usual dolphin friends, being neither a *Delphinus* nor a *Tursiops*. He was identified in his lifetime as a Risso's Dolphin (*Grampus griseus*), a beakless species that is known to occur in the Tasman Sea. Yet he is entitled to be considered the foremost of all friendly dolphins, for two reasons: first, because of the extraordinary length of time he consented to be known to man; and second, because he was the first dolphin that ever caused a country to enact a special law for his protection. During a long lifetime he was seen by many hundreds of tourists from overseas who often made the Nelson crossing specially, articles about him appeared in all the well-known magazines, and he became known all over the world through picture postcards that showed his form rather indistinctly and described him as 'The only fish in the world protected by Act of Parliament'. He even figured among the 'Personal Items' in one of the local newspapers, as a local personality who had returned to his home after a short absence.

For more than twenty years, from 1888 onwards, Pelorus Jack regularly met and accompanied the ships that crossed Cook Strait, between the two main islands of New Zealand, on the run between Wellington and Nelson. He did this over a certain stretch of water off Pelorus Sound and nowhere else, at all times of the day and in the night as well. He would join the Nelson-bound steamer near the entrance to Pelorus Sound and travel with it as far as French Pass, a narrow passage separating D'Urville Island from the South Island mainland. Or he would do the same in the reverse direction, starting just north of the Pass and rarely going beyond a certain point that seemed to mark his limits. It seems that whenever he heard the sound of a ship's engines he would leave off hunting for his food and come to swim by the ship for a while, leaping and riding in the bow-wave and actually rubbing himself against the plates. He would stay alongside for about twenty minutes, or six miles, and then, with a frisk of his tail, be off again.

Among those still living, one of the first to see Pelorus Jack was Mr George Wallace Webber, whose father farmed French Pass at that time and had a contract with the Post Office to board the steamers once a week for the district's mail. This contract began in 1887, and it was when young George Webber came home from school in 1888 that the 'big white fish', as it was called at first, began to be talked about by the passengers and crew of the steamers that used the Pass.

A few years later the Webbers boarded the steamers twice a week, and saw him frequently themselves; and it was about then, says Mr Webber, that someone gave him the name 'Pelorus Jack', presumably following a whaling practice. (In *Moby Dick* there is reference to a whale of these waters that was known as 'New Zealand Jack'.)

'Jack frequently met the steamers coming from Nelson at Collinet Point, commonly known as the Pass Point,' Mr Webber has written, 'and accompanied them for several miles toward Cape Francis, locally known as Clay Point, the northern extremity of Admiralty Bay. He was rarely seen beyond there. His playground seemed to be the six miles across Admiralty Bay from Collinet Point to Cape Francis, where he played round the steamers coming and going between Wellington and Nelson. He never, to my knowledge, went through the Pass. When we were boarding the steamers off Collinet Point and Jack was there, he seemed to be impatient of the steamer waiting, and dived to and fro underneath her, sometimes coming up under our small open boat and giving us a bad jolt. Or he would swim up so close to us that my father used to tell me to give him a push with boathook or oar to keep him off, as he could so easily capsize us. My father used to say he must think we were a large barnacle on the side of the ship which he was trying to rub off.

'As our rowboat was only about thirteen or fourteen feet long, it was a good yardstick to measure Pelorus Jack when he came alongside. He was not as long as our boat, and my father and I estimated that he was between eleven and twelve feet long.

'He was a short heavy mammal, with a small dorsal fin, small side flukes, a strong whale's tail, and pale grey in colour shaded to white underneath. He had a thick rounded head, not at all like the dolphins or blackfish that also abounded in Admiralty Bay. When he was late for the steamer that we were boarding, we would hear the passengers say, "Here he comes!" and I would look up and see Pelorus Jack approaching at racing speed with great leaps and bounds out of the water, often ending close by with a mighty splash. This delighted the passengers.'

This same delight can be felt in the fifty and more letters that I have beside me, from people mostly now in their old age, describing how Pelorus Jack appeared from the decks of the *Arahura*, the *Pateena*, the *Mapourika*, or the ill-fated *Penguin*. Here is the description of Mrs C. Blair, of Nelson:

'A fellow passenger called out "Here comes Pelorus Jack!" and we all thronged to the bow of the ship to see a large silvery-white fish plunging through the waves towards us. As it reached the vessel it turned with it, scraping its body first on one side and then on the other, playfully plunging and springing from the waves. . . . I saw him the last time in March 1910 when my husband and I admired and watched him together. The actions of "Jack" were the same, and in imagination I can still see the lovely graceful creature with the sun shining and gleaming upon his silvery body plunging towards us as we stood and watched from the old ship *Mapourika*.'

There seems no doubt that he actually rubbed against the ship. Ten letters describe this action, from sightings scattered over many years. He 'rubbed himself across the bow', he 'slipped astern, allowing the ship to rub against him', he 'seemed to scrape himself under the keel'. According to Captain R. J. Hay, a veteran master of the Nelson run, 'he used to get around the bow and rub against the ship, I think to clean himself'. And according to another seaman correspondent he swam alongside 'in a kind of snuggling-up attitude'.*

To those who saw him by daylight, Pelorus Jack was

* See page 93.

'light grey with long scratches all over his back' . . . white or cream, a little darker on the upper side' . . . 'patchy white, light grey and dark grey' . . . 'the same dark colour as a porpoise' . . . 'mottled grey-cream, with deep irregular patches, almost yellow'. Or, as one observer puts it, 'He looked old.'

Because he was seen from above he seemed to keep up with the ship (at fifteen knots) without any effort at all. Sometimes he turned on his side, presenting his belly to the ship, and then, one passenger noted, he showed an eye that 'looked almost human'.

To see him on a night crossing was no less wonderful than to see him by day. 'If you can visualise', writes old Mr Fred Barltrop ('Bosun Barltrop' to his Nelson friends in those days), 'a mass of phosphorescent fire fourteen feet in length, travelling through the water with the greatest of ease, then suddenly leaping into the air, the spray and dripping water from him giving one the impression of innumerable fine flashes of electricity, you will get some idea of what Jack looked like.'

In the late nineties and early 1900s, Pelorus Jack was such a regular attendant on the steamers that tourists from abroad actually made the return trip to Nelson specially to see him, and were seldom disappointed. Some, on the other hand (and this is usually said of Americans), would not believe the 'fish story' at any price, and refused to go to the bow with all the rest when the cry of 'Here he comes!' went up.

According to Mr Webber he would meet any steamer that came, but if two were near at the same time he would always leave the slow one for the faster. Thus the *Arahura* and *Pateena*, both twin-screw vessels capable of fifteen knots, came to be favoured by him. He could easily swim much faster than any of the steamers and, says Mr Webber, 'the faster the boat the greater the fun'.

His habit of joining and leaving at a particular spot led to an amusing piece of deception by certain captains. It is said that on approaching the spot they would blow the ship's whistle, pretending to call Pelorus Jack, and 'some persons', says one published account, 'were induced to believe this'. And yet, if this was done, who was being deceived – the passengers, or the captain himself? Did Pelorus Jack learn to come when whistled?

At some point during those years (the date seems uncertain) someone on board one of the steamers fired at Pelorus Jack with a rifle. So far as is known he was not hit, but the result was a demand that he should be protected by law. The demand was strengthened by the belief that museums in Europe would have paid large sums for the animal's body, and that this might tempt some person to kill him for gain.

To make any regulation legally effective it was essential to identify the dolphin's species, and there was difficulty over this for a few years. Information about the various possible species was hard to obtain in New Zealand then, accurate observations of Pelorus Jack were harder still, and for a time, because of his whiteness, he was considered to be a beluga, or white whale. But the beluga has no dorsal fin, and Pelorus Jack undoubtedly had one. As cameras became commoner and more people caught the right moment for an exposure, a range of photographs became available, some clearly showing the tail, some the head, and some the whole outline under the water. One showed him on his side.

At last in 1904 the identification was decided on – apparently by the Rev. D. C. Bates, of the Meteorological Office, Wellington. The length of Pelorus Jack, the shape of his head and mouth, the dorsal fin, and the outline of his tail agreed with the known facts about Risso's Dolphin. The question of colour still presented a problem, since the accounts varied from one another, and especially from what was then recorded of Risso's Dolphin. Because this species was believed to have the dark back common to most dolphins, it was considered that Pelorus Jack must be an albino, like Moby Dick himself, and therefore an outcast – which conveniently explained his apparent isolation from the herd, and his taking to the company of ships.

Dr F. C. Fraser writes in *Giant Fishes, Whales, and Dolphins* that the colouring of Risso's Dolphin is 'grey, which on the fins and tail deepens to black, and on the undersurface becomes much lighter or even white'. There is no sharp line dividing light and dark, he says, and 'very commonly the skin is scored with long narrow white marks – a most conspicuous feature when they are present'. These marks have been explained by some as the scars of wounds inflicted by the parrot-like beak of the cuttle-fish, which the stomach contents of stranded specimens have shown to be the principal diet of Risso's Dolphin, and there is no doubt that Pelorus Jack had marks of this kind.

The slight discrepancies in the various descriptions of Pelorus Jack's colouring can be readily accounted for. Fleeting glimpses caught under conditions of excitement were inevitably subjective, and become all the more so when remembered in old age. But it is also now known that Risso's Dolphin, like man himself, turns grey with age, and the observer who in 1905 thought that Pelorus Jack 'looked old' was nearer the mark than he realised.

At all events, it was as Risso's Dolphin that Pelorus Jack was protected in 1904, not by an 'Act of Parliament' as the postcards said, but by an Order in Council, signed by the Governor of the Colony, Lord Plunket. From the wording it is clear that the Governor had, in fact, no authority at all under the Seafisheries Act to prohibit the taking of aquatic mammals. The Act gave him powers relating only to fish. So the law prevaricates, and Pelorus Jack becomes a 'fish or mammal'. The regulation would have failed in court, had it ever been put to the test; but the entire population of New Zealand would have deplored the fact.

Prohibiting Taking of Risso's Dolphin in Cook Strait, &c.

———

[signed] PLUNKET

Governor

ORDER IN COUNCIL

At the Government House, at Wellington, this twenty-sixth day of September, 1904

Present:

HIS EXCELLENCY THE GOVERNOR IN COUNCIL

WHEREAS it is enacted by section five of 'The Sea-fisheries Act, 1894', that the Governor in Council may from time to time make regulations, which shall have general force and effect throughout the colony, or particular force and effect only in any waters or places specified therein, for, among other things, prohibiting altogether for such period as he shall think fit the taking of any fish, and may by such regulations impose a penalty for breach of such regulations:

And whereas it is desirable to prohibit the taking of the fish or mammal known as Risso's dolphin (*Grampus griseus*) in Cook Strait and the adjacent bays, sounds, and estuaries:

Now, therefore, His Excellency the Governor of the Colony of New Zealand, in exercise of the hereinbefore-recited power and authority, and acting by and with the advice and consent of the Executive Council of the said colony, doth hereby make the following regulations: –

REGULATIONS

1. During the period of five years from the date of the gazetting of these regulations it shall not be lawful for any person to take the fish or mammal of the species commonly known as Risso's dolphin (*Grampus griseus*) in the waters of Cook Strait, or of the bays, sounds, and estuaries adjacent thereto.

2. Any person committing a breach of this regulation shall be liable to a penalty of not less than five pounds nor more than one hundred pounds.

ALEX. WILLIS
Clerk of the Executive Council*

When this Order in Council was first made, Pelorus Jack had been keeping his station with the steamers for fifteen years, and it was twice renewed before he finally disappeared.

It had been in force for four years when a new witness

* From the *New Zealand Gazette*, September 26, 1904.

in the story of Pelorus Jack came on the scene. It was in 1908 that Mr Charlie Moeller, of the Marine Department's lighthouse service, was appointed keeper of the light at French Pass and began an acquaintance with the dolphin that lasted until the end. Although I have reason to doubt his memory on certain crucial points, Mr Moeller makes a good story of *his* Pelorus Jack, and what follows is from a tape-recorded interview.

'I was on the lookout for him from the first day,' says Mr Moeller, 'because of course he was the talk of the country at that time, always spoken about. One night I woke up – it wasn't a watched light at French Pass, I just got up occasionally, every four hours as a rule; if you woke in time, well and good, and if you didn't, it didn't matter, you just got up occasionally. I heard a row down below my house, I couldn't make out what it was, splashing and tearing around. I got out of bed and went and had a look, and it was this Pelorus Jack. I didn't know it was then, but it was him all right. He was catching his tea! He used to eat cod – small cod. I watched him catch them, tearing around just under the house, and he wouldn't go away. You couldn't sleep. He used to blow just like a whale – he was a species of whale – and he used to come up and blow, and then he'd go down and get some more fish. My wife was annoyed about it. She said: "You'll have to do something about this fish kicking up a row all night, keeping the youngsters awake." So I got some stones and threw them at him, and away he went. That was my first introduction to Pelorus Jack.'

Over the next four years Charlie Moeller became pretty familiar with the dolphin, and he bears out what Mr Webber and various sea-captains have said – that

Pelorus Jack never went *through* French Pass, but always lived on the Wellington side, and left the south-bound steamers at the Pass.

He noticed that not only could Pelorus Jack detect the presence of a ship from far away, but he seemed able to distinguish between two ships and make his choice. If two vessels were in the offing and he was between them, Mr Moeller says, 'he would pause, and you could almost read his thoughts. Then he'd always go to the nearest one.'

Others have said that he never bothered with 'oil launches', as they were called in those days, or with yachts, but was attracted only to steamers, and presumably by some sound that they made.

What sound? By the ordinary mechanical noises of the engines? Or by some ultrasonic vibrations created by steam under pressure? Or is there, perhaps, some other sound that is characteristic of ships and attractive to dolphins? I do not know whether Risso's Dolphin makes the 'rusty hinge' noise that is characteristic of *Tursiops*, but it is amusing to think that the creaking noises we hear from our bunks when a ship takes the swell may be accompanied by ultrasonic overtones that a dolphin would hear.

Mr Moeller's explanation for the dolphin's habit of rubbing against the ship is surprising. 'It tore those barnacles off him,' he says.

There are in fact some kinds of barnacle that attach themselves to the larger whales, and although I can find no record of Risso's Dolphin having them, Mr Moeller asserts that Pelorus Jack did.

'It was the speed of the boat coming, and he always

came in alongside of the boat and then gradually dropped astern just a little way,' he says. 'The speed of the boat was faster than him and it tore those barnacles off him. It was the irritation, he was getting scratched, that's what happened. Of course people didn't believe that. They came from Europe, and they came from England and America and every time there were tourists who came to see this wonderful fish. They all thought he was a pilot, that he was piloting the boats through, but I don't think he ever did that. He was in constant irritation, that was what was wrong with him.'

There was another interesting piece of animal behaviour that Mr Moeller and a friend of his observed. The friend used to take a dog in his dinghy when he went fishing near the Pass. Pelorus Jack would come up to the dinghy and curve around it in his usual manner, and the dog would leap about and bark, and try to bite him. Would a dog bark at a fish, if a fish were to behave in the same way? Or is there something about a dolphin – something about its 'human-looking' eye – that a dog recognises and wants to bark at?

In March 1911 the dead body of a dolphin was washed up on D'Urville Island. It resembled Pelorus Jack except that it was black (it was probably a young one of the same species) and the report went out that the 'famous fish' was dead. This appeared in all the papers on March 21. But immediately there were denials from the crew of the *Pateena*, who said that they had seen him as usual, and 'never so frisky'.

It was a little more than a year later, when he had been at his station for nearly twenty-four years, that Pelorus Jack went missing for the last time. For years afterwards there were all sorts of rumours and theories about the reason for his disappearance, and it is a measure of the general feeling of wonder that surrounded the phenomenon that, away from French Pass itself, every explanation was thought of except the simple one of death from old age.

There had already been the popular story that he would never go near the ship from which he had been fired at; and it was this ship – reputed to be the *Penguin* – that sank on February 12, 1909, with the loss of seventy-five lives. There was also the story (conflicting with Mr Webber's observation) that he kept away from twin-screw vessels because he had been struck by one of the propellers when they first came on the run.

After his final disappearance it was said by some that he had 'gone through the Pass' for the first time and the last time. The local Maoris no doubt had some other explanation – perhaps that Ruru had at last been freed from his curse. But the story that had the widest circulation was that Pelorus Jack had fallen victim to the harpoons of a small fleet of Norwegian whalers which is known to have anchored off the entrance to Pelorus Sound about April 20, 1912. The crew were 'foreigners' of course – like the wicked Thracians, 'unkind and surely greatly sinful', whom Oppian condemns. Knowing nothing of the Order in Council, they had doubtless acted in a manner that would have been unthinkable to New Zealanders, and 'boiled him down for oil'.

Two who did not feel it necessary to look for any mysterious explanation were Mr Webber and Mr Moeller. 'It is my own impression that he was an old fish,' Mr Webber has written, 'and died from natural causes.' And

Mr Moeller has his own tale to tell. He believes that the body of a dolphin which he found not long after April 1912 was that of Pelorus Jack.

I shall give Mr Moeller's version here, without asserting that it settles the matter. I have not been able to travel about the country interviewing the various elderly people whose information, when pooled and checked with old ship's logs, might lead to certainty. There are one or two points in Mr Moeller's story that do not fit in with other known or accepted facts, and it may be that doubt will only be removed – if it ever is – after the publication of this book. Here is his story:

One day at slack water Mr Moeller was working on the outside beacon at the Pass – the one on the reef on the D'Urville side – when he saw 'a grey thing floating'. It was most unusual for anything to *float* through French Pass. The undertow was so great that when any object like a log or a piece of jetsam got into the current 'it upended and went down, and you never saw it again until it came up three miles away towards Nelson or towards Wellington'.

'I thought, this was funny, this thing floating down here like this, so I went and got into my boat and went out and alongside, and waited for him to come alongside of me. The fish came down, and immediately I saw him I thought to myself, "This is Pelorus Jack, nothing else." He was the size, he was the colour, he was everything that I had seen for the last four years, every day.

'I made him fast to the painter. I had an old piece of rope, and I put it round his tail and pulled him to the shore. My boatway was just about fifty yards further down, and I just towed him in and put him in there, brought him in to the boatway. And I began to think then, "This is Pelorus Jack all right, there's nothing surer in the world." I knew he was protected by Order in Council, and it was my job, I was responsible for anything like that in connection with the Government, I was there for that purpose as well as the light. It was interesting to the Government, so I went straight to my house and wired Wellington, to the secretary of the Marine Department, Mr Allport, and told him.

'Next thing I knew, the Government steamer *Hinemoa* steamed through the Pass, and a boatload came ashore – the curator of the Wellington Museum I saw it was, and Mr Allport, and some others. I didn't know the others, I've forgotten their names and who they were. I was introduced to them but that was about all.

'They all gathered round the fish. They seemed to refer everything to Captain Bollons, the captain of the *Hinemoa*. Being a nautical man, I suppose they thought he was the right man. They talked it over, one passed one opinion, one another, and they measured him, his girth and his length. He was just a couple of inches over the fourteen feet, and it was recognised and known or put down that Pelorus Jack was fourteen feet.

'Captain Bollons measured him and so did Mr Allport, and they talked it over amongst themselves. I was standing back, and Captain Bollons came over to me then, and he said, "Well, Charlie – it's not Pelorus Jack."

'I said, "Are you sure?"

'He said, "Yes, I'm sure," and I said, "Well, I'm certain. It's Pelorus Jack all right, and you can't tell me anything different, I've known and seen him too often. Not once but hundreds of times, every day since I've been staying here."

'Well, he said, "No, it's not Pelorus Jack. The colour's wrong, the length's wrong, everything's wrong."

'I said, "Oh well, Captain, you pass the verdict. I thought I was just doing the right thing." He never said anything, and he went over to Mr Allport, and then he came back and said, "Oh well, Charlie, on behalf of the Government we all know we can commend you for doing your job, but you'll see Pelorus Jack again doing *his* job, and he'll be alongside the next steamer that comes through."

'It was the *Hinemoa* – she was on the southern side – and Pelorus Jack *wasn't* there. I never heard any more about it,* and he was never seen afterwards. *He was never seen again.*'

On the next tide, Mr Moeller says, the carcase floated off the boatway and was washed up on the beach on the D'Urville side. He fetched a Norwegian fisherman of the district, named Galzell, and this man agreed that it was Pelorus Jack. But they left the carcase there, and it rotted on the beach.

'And do you know,' says Charlie Moeller, 'the Order in Council came into force for the simple reason that there were so many people wanting to get hold of him. The museum in Berlin wanted him, and the museum in Vienna wanted him, and they were frightened that somebody might shoot him, for his body was worth a lot, and that's why they protected him. But I missed the chance of a lifetime. I just let him rot away – I was that confounded wild.'

---

* I can find no record in the files of the New Zealand Marine Department of any visit by the *Hinemoa* at this time, nor was it entered in the lighthouse log.

Opononi

❀   ❀   ❀   ❀

The world marvelled at the story of Pelorus Jack, but the stories from the ancient world continued to be regarded as fables – that is, by the few who knew of them. In London in 1929 the Linnean Society completed an informal inquiry into the history and habits of Pelorus Jack, which was reported at its annual meeting. The president at that time was Sir Sidney Harmer, himself an authority on whales. 'In the light of this story,' Harmer said, 'we may have to review our incredulity in regard to the classical narratives of the friendliness of dolphins towards mankind.' Nine years later, with the establishment of Marine Studios in Florida, the review of our incredulity began in earnest. But it was only in 1956, at Opononi, that a *wild* dolphin produced the final vindication of the Greek and Roman tales.

Opononi, as I said at the beginning, is a small township just inside the mouth of the Hokianga Harbour, on the western side of the north island of New Zealand, near its top end. Hokianga is a Maori name of course (but Opononi, though it looks like one, is not; its origin is unexplained), and there are many Maori families in the district, descended from the original tribes. At Opononi the road to the far north runs along the harbour's edge, with a sandy beach below it and just enough room for the township between the road and the hills. There is the white-and-green hotel,* built of wood in the old colonial

* No longer so. It has since been burnt down.

style, with its long verandah stepping straight onto the road; and a post office, a service station, a store, and a milk-bar. There is not much else to the place except the wooden Memorial Hall, and the motor-camp, where holiday-makers pitch their tents or caravans beneath the pine trees at Christmas time.

Unlike much of the New Zealand landscape, the surrounding scene has a calm and peaceful character. The hills around the harbour are soft in outline and in colour. Across the water from Opononi, the end of the peninsula that comes down from the north to enclose the harbour appears to consist of nothing but sand – high hills of it, of a tender, salmon-pink colour, as if they were part of the sunset. Even the Aegean could hardly provide a lovelier setting for a dolphin legend.

If there is anything that Opononi has in common with Iasos, Poroselene, and Hippo, you will have noticed it by now. It is sometimes said of oysters that they should only be eaten when there is an R in the month, and it pleases me to think that dolphins prefer to make their human friendships in places whose names contain an O, and if possible some other letter out of dolphin, too: Miletos and Tainaron, Iasos, Poroselene, Puteoli, Hippo, Narbonne, Motutapu, and Pelorus Sound. They also seem to like their human friends to have an O, although to this they will make exceptions. Dionysos created them of course, and there was Arion, and Koiranos, and the boy Dionysios; and who was a better friend to dolphins than Oppian? As to the nicknames they are given for themselves, Pliny says they prefer Simo to any other, but I think the main thing they ask for is the O. So the little town of Opononi – no letter not in dolphin – was surely bound to receive a visit from a dolphin some day. And five years ago it came about.

Early in 1955 the boat-owners of the Hokianga began to take notice of a creature which at first they thought was a shark, because of its one black fin. After they had seen it several times they realised that it was following their boats, and soon they knew it was not a shark, but a dolphin.

Not long before this there had been an incident which people remembered later. Some stupid youth with a rifle had fired at a family of these animals cruising near the shore, and boasted of having shot one. So when the fishermen became familiar with that single black fin in the harbour they possibly were meeting a young dolphin that had lost its mother. It was subsequently learned that the dolphin would have been about one year old at that time.

Before long the whole district knew of the dolphin. People fishing on the harbour began to seek it out, and the dolphin in turn came closer to the boats, out of what seemed to be curiosity. Then someone found that it liked being scratched with an oar, or with a mop. (The launch-owners carried mops to sluice their boats down after cleaning fish.) Gradually it began to follow the boats to the wharf and the beach, and as the summer came round again the dolphin began to make the acquaintance of humans in the water. But it kept its distance, and for some time no one got very close to it.

It would glide in near the beach when people were bathing, moving its dark body with gentle undulations of its tail just under the surface. From the wharf at Opononi you can see straight to the sandy bottom, and the children

are all accustomed to watching the pale blue shapes of kingfish chasing sprats between the wooden piles. But no one was accustomed to seeing a large black animal like a shark, fully eight feet long, nosing about in that same water without causing all the swimmers to rush for safety.

Who touched the dolphin first? Thanks to Piwai Toi, it is possible to answer that question. After the Opononi dolphin had become as famous as Pelorus Jack, Mr Toi wrote an article about it for *Te Ao Hou* (*The New World*), a quarterly magazine published for the Maori people by the New Zealand Government. I should explain that by then the dolphin had become generally known by the nickname 'Opo', having first been known as 'Opononi Jack'. It was also known that she was a female. She was a young *Tursiops*, about three-quarters grown. Mr Toi, who describes himself as 'just a hardworking Maori farmer who was born in the Opononi district', had not written anything of this kind before, and you will notice that his writing is like a translation from the Greek. This is how he described the dolphin:

'Although I had heard that there was a dolphin in the Hokianga Harbour I did not make her acquaintance until June of 1955. I was returning from Rangi Point School about 6.30 p.m. and the sea was rather choppy. Suddenly there was a big splash and a boiling swirl. A large fish was streaking for my boat just under the surface. I really thought it was going to hit my boat, when about ten yards away it dived and surfaced on the other side. It played round and round the boat. Such was the way I first met Opo. I was afraid she would be hit by my outboard, so I went inshore as close as I could. When I was in about four feet of water I looked back. She was about three feet out

B.D.—P

of the water, standing literally on her tail and looking at me from a distance of about fifty yards away. She sank out of sight and that was the last I saw of her that afternoon.'

The next time Mr Toi and the dolphin met, she did what the *taniwha* did for Te Whare's father after Te Whare had been thrown out of the canoe:

'In August of the same year, two other chaps and I went to Rangi Point to gather *pipis*. We had not gone far when we were joined by Opo. By this time, whenever we went out fishing we were always on the lookout for her and rarely were we disappointed. Opo really gave a charming display that day. She played round and round our boat and then swam just under the keel. When she did this you could feel the boat being lifted in the swell she made as she swam under the boat.

'One of the chaps sat right in the bow and kept putting his hand in the sea trying to touch Opo. At last he did. As far as I know he was the first person to touch Opo with his hand. While we were picking *pipis*, three boats passed going to Opononi, but she stayed just out from our boat cruising round. Then she followed us all the way back to Opononi.'

By Christmas of 1955, when the annual invasion of summer visitors to the Hokianga was in full swing, the dolphin could be depended on to appear almost every day, and if she was away when people wanted to see her, she could easily be sent for. She would always come to the summons of an outboard motor, or the cheerful *putt-putt* of a launch. She had, in Mr Toi's words, 'a real weakness for the sound of an outboard motor'.

'Once she heard the motor she followed just like a dog,

playing or cruising round the boat. As soon as she arrived, people swarmed to the wharf and the beach, taking snaps, marvelling, or just enjoying themselves watching her. In fact I have felt sorry for her as she never seemed to have the time to feed during the day. If she had an urge to wander, an outboard had only to be started and she would return to her admirers again.'

That she could hear the sound from far away Mr Toi had good reason to know: 'Many times I have gone to watch the people playing on the beach with Opo. I would be about a quarter of a mile away with the motor idling when I would hear "Oh!" from her admirers on the beach. Next thing I would see Opo coming towards me. Many times I have rowed away from Opononi and started my motor only to find Opo had left her admirers and was following my boat, but I always returned her to the beach and then by rowing a long way off before starting my motor I could leave her to her friends.'

By the New Year, thousands of people were coming to Opononi specially to see the dolphin. People who had planned to spend their holidays camping in the north decided to camp at Opononi – if there was room. But the motor-camp was full, and the hotel was booked for months ahead. At the week-ends, Opononi had such crowds on its narrow bit of road between the village and the beach as had never been seen before in that part of New Zealand. The stores rang up for truckloads of ice-cream and soft drinks, and the hotel sent for a lot more beer.

It was all so like what happened at Hippo seventeen centuries before, and yet in one respect so different. Far from beginning to exhaust 'the modest resources of the town', the crowds of trippers arriving from north and south were a gladdening sight, at least to the business people. And so, remembering the rifle shots of fools, they formed a committee for the dolphin's protection. They put up signs by the roadside. 'WELCOME TO OPONONI, BUT DON'T TRY TO SHOOT OUR GAY GOLPHIN' said the signs, using a nickname the children had given her.

But Piwai Toi can convey the atmosphere of those days far better than I:

'One of my daughters had to work at week-ends, as the proprietor of the tearooms was unable to cope with the crowds,' he writes. 'We asked our daughter how many people were there each day and she said round about fifteen hundred to two thousand. We were a bit sceptical so we went to Opononi one Sunday afternoon, just out of idle curiosity. If I had not seen it for myself I would never have believed it. I have heard of traffic jams and crowded beaches, but to see them at Opononi was a wonderful experience. This did not happen once or twice but every Saturday and Sunday. Cars, buses, trucks, vans, and motor-bikes were seen parked on either side of the road for half a mile or more on each side of Opononi, with barely room to drive along the centre of the road. If a vehicle was held up or was to meet one coming the opposite way a traffic jam was the immediate result. Traffic was so congested at times that officers had to be brought in to direct it. Two officers were on duty most Sundays, and they did a very good job in untangling traffic.'

On this mass of sunburned, jostling humanity, the gentle dolphin had the effect of a benediction. Saturdays, for all the crowds and all the beer, were not as New Zealand Saturdays so often are, and Mr Toi noticed it: 'With all these people coming during the week-end,' he writes, 'Saturdays in particular when up to fifteen hundred people were jammed on the beach, there was no case of drunkenness, fights, or arguments. Everybody was in the gayest of holiday moods.'

As at Iasos and Hippo, so in the Hokianga: first rights to the dolphin's friendship were accorded to the children, both by the grown-ups and by the dolphin herself. Notices were put up near the wharf asking visitors not to spoil the children's enjoyment, while 'As for herself,' writes Mr Toi, 'she was really and truly a children's playmate. Although she played with grown-ups she was really at her charming best with a crowd of children swimming and wading. I have seen her swimming amongst children almost begging to be petted. She had an uncanny knack of finding out those who were gentle among her young admirers, and keeping away from the rougher elements. If they were all gentle then she would give of her best.'

Again, this New World dolphin made a favourite of one particular child. Her choice was a girl, whose name is Jill Baker. Jill was thirteen years old at the time and a keen swimmer, and living as she did right on the main road at Opononi she was always in the water. In spite of having no O in her name she was favoured by the dolphin. When she was fourteen she wrote for this book the following description:

'I think why the dolphin became so friendly with me was because I was always gentle with her and never rushed at her as so many bathers did. No matter how many went in the water playing with her, as soon as I went in for a swim she would leave all the others and go off side-by-side with me. I remember on one occasion I went for a swim much further up the beach than where she was playing, and I was only in the water a short while when she bobbed up just in front of my face and gave me such a fright. On several other occasions when I was standing in the water with my legs apart she would go between them and pick me up and carry me a short distance before dropping me again. At first she didn't like the feel of my hands and would dart away, but after a while when she realised that I would not harm her she would come up to me to be rubbed and patted. She would quite often let me put little children on her back for a moment or two.'

The dolphin's feeding grounds were in the shallow waters further up the harbour, where there were plenty of snapper and mullet. From there, if there was no crowd demanding her presence at the wharf, she would sometimes follow a boat toward the heads. But she would never go beyond a certain rock, which seemed to mark her harbour limits. If she ever went outside the harbour to the open sea, no one knew about it. Now and then she did disappear for a day or so.

Sometimes the fishermen returning with their catch tried to feed her. They offered her mullet, and no doubt other fish as well, but she would never take it. She might have done so had they known that in order to 'show' a food fish to a wild dolphin you need to slap it on the water and then hold it below the surface.

As she grew more used to the animals with pink legs, the dolphin began to play delightful games. Someone gave her a coloured beach ball, and she quickly discovered how to toss it high out of the water with the tip of her snout. While it was spinning through the air she would race forward to be under it when it fell. But let us hear Piwai Toi describe these games:

'When playing with a rubber ball no one could help being thrilled by her antics with it. She would push the ball along the water and then flip it in the air, catch it on her nose, then toss it in the air again, or she would try and sink the ball by pressing it under her body or tail. She must have got it fairly deep at times as the ball bounced nearly four feet up in the air when it escaped from under her. Then she would toss it in the air and hit it with her tail.

'Then there was her game of playing with empty beer bottles. Toss her a beer bottle, empty or full, and she would treat it with disdain.* She had to find her own beer bottle from the bottom of the sea. How she balanced it on her nose I cannot imagine but she really did and she would toss it quite a distance up in the air.

'I have tried to make her play with a glass ball, a float from a seine net, but she never seems to use it which makes me think she could not see anything clear like glass. She even tried to toss a piece of brown paper which I threw overboard.'

It was noticed that the dolphin seemed both to hear and enjoy the laughter of the crowd, and the people were sure she liked an audience. When one of her tricks had produced a cry of approval she would make an exultant leap, high out of the water, showing all her gleaming lines in the sunlight. But she never did this when bathers or children were near. Like the dolphins at Narbonne, she was always gentle in the presence of her human friends.

* It should be remembered that this is Polynesia, and in Polynesia a *full* beer bottle would not be considered wasted on the dolphin.

As time went by, more and more of them learned how, to get close without making her shy away. The school-teacher, Mrs Goodson, was photographed holding her head up out of the water. Some of the visitors, even, were able to boast that she had swum between their legs. Others, especially the amateur photographers, had sore shins to remember her by. She was probably merely curious; the photographer who took the pictures of Opo in this book more than once felt her trying to lift his foot off the bottom with her snout.

At times, when the crowds were at their greatest, the dolphin had reason to be annoyed. There were people who would insist on clutching at her flippers or her tail, and would try to turn her over or prevent her going past. When apparently displeased she would move out of reach, *without haste*, but smacking her tail flat on the water every few yards as she went. Her annoyance never took a stronger form than this.

One morning there was an accident. The dolphin had followed the fishing launch *Sonoma* to the wharf, where a cluster of people were waiting to buy the catch. She came too close to the boat, and was struck by the turning propeller. She made off in a flurry, and the launch-owner found the water coloured with blood. She was not seen again that day, and everyone shared the alarm the launch-man felt. Next morning when the launch set off with passengers, there was a cry from the bow, and the dolphin appeared, flashing across the water. She leapt out twice to her full height, displaying all her easy strength, and then came alongside, to reveal two gashes near her head. Everyone on board was certain she had done it to re-assure them; and in fact it was impossible not to believe that the dolphin had feelings towards her human friends, like those they had for her.

It was strange how everyone wanted to touch the dolphin. 'Some people got so excited when they saw Opo,' writes Mr Toi, 'that they went into the water fully clothed, just to touch her.' Often it must have suggested some Biblical scene, with simple believers crowding to touch the garment of a Holy prophet and gain redemption. Those who succeeded found eager listeners afterwards while they described nothing more than what she felt like. One said the fin was like smooth vulcanite. Another said the skin along her side was like hard dry suede. In the evenings, when it was too chilly to be in the water any longer and the dolphin had gone off, everyone talked about her. In the tents that glowed like pale green lanterns under the pine-trees, the campers exchanged their scanty knowledge of the marvel, speaking in low voices while the children slept. They visited each other's tents, becoming friends with total strangers in an instant, all because of the dolphin. And in the hotel dining-room, everyone talked to everyone. There was such an overflow of these friendly feelings that it seemed the crowds were composed of people wanting to be forgiven for something – for the unkindness, perhaps, that humans generally do to animals in the wild. The dolphin, who never once snapped at a hand, seemed to offer forgiveness for all.

Perhaps the most memorable of all her days was that of the Opononi School picnic, held soon after the schools began again in February. The children were all in the water, and the dolphin was lazing around among them, when someone had the idea of forming the children in a ring. They all held hands, and the dolphin, as if she understood precisely, circled round inside the ring, and someone threw her a beach ball. Gently she tossed it in the air, as she was expected to, and then she left the ring again. This happy moment was captured on film for anyone to see.

Throughout the country there was the feeling that this dolphin should be given the same protection by law as had been given fifty years earlier to Pelorus Jack, and the Government arranged to do this. In the first week of March it was made known that the 'Fisheries (Dolphin Protection) Regulations, 1956' would become law in a few days' time. They were passed, like the previous regulations, by an Order in Council, made in the presence of the Governor-General.

'During the period of five years from the commencement of these regulations,' the Order in Council said, 'it shall not be lawful for any person to take or molest any dolphin in the Hokianga Harbour, being all that area of tidal land and tidal water inside the seaward arc of a circle having a radius of two nautical miles from the Signal Station on the South Head at the entrance to the said harbour. Any person committing a breach of these regulations shall be liable on summary conviction to a fine not exceeding £50.'

These regulations were gazetted on Thursday, March 8, 1956, and they became law at twelve o'clock that night.

०   ०   ०   ०

Had the dolphin remained, and come to no harm, there would have been great changes at Opononi. In Roman Africa, where custom demanded that the town should entertain important visitors without being repaid, it was necessary to have the dolphin secretly put to death. At

Opononi, there was talk of a new wing being added to the hotel. Pelorus Jack had kept his station in Cook Strait for twenty-two years. Might not that happen at Opononi?

On that very Thursday, however, on which the regulation became law, Opo failed to arrive in her usual way. She had been playing among the bathers the day before, and some fishermen had seen her in the morning, but when a boat went to fetch her for Mr James Fitzpatrick's cameras in the afternoon, she could not be found. For the first twenty-four hours no one worried overmuch. She had been known to do this before.

On the Friday, four boats searched the length of the harbour for her without success. And at noon that day an elderly Maori who was collecting mussels at low tide found her dead body. It was jammed in a crevice between some rocks at Koutu Point, five miles up harbour, where she had evidently been feeding. The tide had gone out, leaving her trapped in a pool, with the crevice her only escape. Some of her skin was scraped off along one side, apparently by her struggles to get through the crevice to the sea.

What had caused her to die in this manner? It is unthinkable that, with all her instinctive knowledge of the tides, she would let herself get trapped in the pool through carelessness. It could be that her echo-location system became confused, but I fear it is more likely that she was trapped in the pool because, either accidentally or deliberately, she had been hurt. Some of the people who live around the Hokianga are given to the habit of doing their fishing with explosives. If someone was using gelignite to kill snapper in the pool when the dolphin was feeding nearby, she could have been stunned by the blast, and remained unconscious till the tide was out. Or some fool may have done the thing on purpose. If so, he seems to have escaped the timing of the law by a few hours.

Piwai Toi, however, does not think it was any of these things. His explanation is the one that Plutarch would have given, and it is expressed very much in Plutarch's manner – complete with an anatomical mistake:

'My own humble opinion, for what it is worth, is that she committed suicide. I base my conjecture on two points. Opo was a female dolphin and there was no male to keep her company. A dolphin is a mammal and her young are suckled and get their milk from a shallow dent under her flippers where they join her body. As she was a lone dolphin the urge to reproduce like any other animal could not be satisfied. This hankering for young to mother is one reason why she got so friendly with humans, especially with children, also why she liked being stroked with an oar or a mop. Invariably when being stroked she would turn over on her back to be stroked on her stomach. But her greatest urge was for reproduction of her own kind. When this urge was not satisfied she committed suicide by deliberately getting herself stranded.'

When word reached the village that the dolphin was dead, a gloom came over everyone. That evening, as dusk settled over the harbour, her body was towed by a small boat to the beach where she had played so joyfully not long before. A silent crowd received her there, and the body was dragged up the beach and hung from the branch of a tree. Later, with reverence after their fashion, the people buried her beside the Memorial Hall, and covered her grave with flowers.

The news went out to the rest of the world, and in New

Zealand, people who had merely read of the dolphin in their newspapers shared the sorrow that Opononi felt. My own small son, who had never seen her, was a tearful boy that night, and we were all made sad by the ending of the story. From many parts of the country telegrams and letters went to Opononi expressing sympathy, especially to the children, and one of these was from the Governor-General. At Hippo, the Governor of the Province 'poured some precious ointment on the dolphin'. In New Zealand, Sir Willoughby Norrie sent a message of sympathy from Government House.

And now I prefer that it should be Oppian's pen, not mine, that ends our tribute to the gentle dolphin:

'This other excellent deed of the dolphins have I heard and admire. When fell disease and fatal draws nigh to them, they fail not to know it but are aware of the end of life. Then they flee the sea and the wide waters of the deep and come aground on the shallow shores. And there they give up their breath and receive their doom upon the land; that so perchance some mortal man may take pity on the holy messenger of Poseidon when he lies low, and cover him with mound of shingle, remembering his gentle friendship; or haply the seething sea herself may hide his body in the sands; nor do any of the brood of the sea behold the corse of their lord, nor any foe do dishonour to his body even in death. Excellence and majesty attend them even when they perish, nor do they shame their glory even when they die.'

How to Help a Stranded Dolphin

What an admirable, useful, and lovable creature, then, is the dolphin! He deserves our respect and affection, and also any help that we can give him whenever we find him in trouble; for sometimes dolphins do get into trouble, and there are opportunities for human beings to rescue them. Like their bigger cousins the Pilot Whales, or Blackfish, as they are usually called, dolphins occasionally get stranded on the shore; and there, either because of overheating if the tide is going out, or because of drowning if it is coming in, they die.

No one has yet discovered why these strandings occur. There is a temptation to suppose that perhaps some ancient 'memory' is at work, driving the creature back to the land on which its ancestors once lived, under an impulse of the sort that sends us humans swimming in the sea. But this notion will hardly stand up in the light of what is understood nowadays about the nature of instinct. The cause is still to be looked for. We do not hear of birds having unexplained forced landings, or of frogs or lizards being mysteriously drowned. Then why do dolphins strand, sometimes in numbers and sometimes alone, and why do they often refuse to accept an opportunity to swim away again when it is given by human help?

When Pilot Whales are stranded it is extremely difficult to move them because of their size and number, and because of this mysterious urge that makes them commit what Plutarch thought was suicide. Dolphins, on the other hand, are smaller and commonly strand themselves in smaller numbers, so it is worth while making the attempt to give them their liberty. Even so, the difficulties may be considerable.

This was the case on Easter Sunday, 1956, when seven dolphins were stranded at a little place called Tryphena, on Great Barrier Island, which is off the northern coast of New Zealand not far from Auckland. Looking out towards the Pacific on a clear day the people of Auckland can see Great Barrier – but only the tops of it. All that shows above the horizon is a line of pale blue mountain peaks like separate islands. The island was given its name because it stands as a barrier shielding the gulf and Auckland's harbour from the ocean rollers of the Pacific. People go there from Auckland for holidays, and at Easter, 1956, some friends of mine who were spending the holiday at Tryphena tried to help the seven stranded dolphins.

It was late on Sunday night, when the moon was just rising behind the island and the tide was going out, that someone came running up with the news that there were dolphins on the beach. My friends rushed down, and there they were, splashing and squeaking on the rocks in shallow water. It was time for bed, but everyone forgot about that. Far into the night, and again from early next morning, my friends with their neighbours and their neighbours' children tried everything they could think of in an effort to save all seven of the animals. They were common dolphins, or *Delphinus delphis*, the prettily marked small kind with the ring-eye and the 'saddle' on their

backs. But when I say 'small', you must remember that a
Common Dolphin is about seven or eight feet long, and it
takes at least two people to handle one of them. In spite of
their efforts, the rescuers did not save all seven. But what
they learned in the attempt may well help you to succeed,
should you ever find dolphins stranded on the shore.

My friend Henry Lambert, as it happens, is a physicist
who knows a good deal about high-frequency sounds, and
before this adventure at Tryphena he knew of the sounds
that dolphins make, and their purpose; even so, he wished
afterwards that he had known still more about the
animals' nature, and especially about the way they behave when in trouble. For, as he realises now, there was a
way by which all seven dolphins might have been saved
that night, if only someone had thought of it at the time.
But this is what happened, from the moment when the
excited cry was heard, 'There's seven dolphins on the
shore!'

At once the Lamberts and their neighbours, Mr Todd
and the Whitfords, all waded in to where the dolphins lay,
curious to see them close at hand and to touch and stroke
them – for something told them there was nothing to fear.
They were amazed to discover that the breath from their
blowholes was warm, and their skin felt smooth, like
plastic. Then someone brought torches, and they saw that
one dolphin was bleeding from the mouth, and another
had a gash on its side. In their struggles the dolphins were
cutting themselves to pieces on the rocks, so everyone
began trying to guide them into deeper water. It was no
use: the 'rescued' ones insisted on returning to their
fellows. (They were being called, presumably, by the dis-
tressful whistling of those that were still on the rocks; the

B.D.—Q

sound was travelling through the shallow water, but even Mr Lambert didn't think at the time of a way to prevent this happening.)

They went on trying, but it was arduous work, struggling with animals so heavy and so hard to grip, and it didn't seem to be getting the dolphins back to safety. After a while, when everyone had spent a good deal of energy in vain, someone had the idea of taking a dolphin some distance out and tethering it so that it *couldn't* come back. It was thought that the others would be attracted to it, and to keep it company they would take two other dolphins too. But this was no good either; two of the men, using a dinghy, did succeed in tethering one dolphin by making a noose around its tail and tying the rope to a heavy concrete anchor, but the other two dolphins came back to their mates on the rocks. Everyone felt discouraged, and by this time tired out. But before they all went home to their beds they gave a last thought to the dolphins. Two, they managed to leave in comparative comfort on the sand; four defied them and remained on the rocks; and the seventh, tethered beyond low-water mark, was still straining at the rope to rejoin its mates when the men left it.

At three o'clock it rained, and Henry Lambert woke. Most of us would have pulled the blankets tighter, but he got out of bed and went to the beach in a raincoat. He managed to drag one of the dolphins that had been left on the sand further down towards the water. Soon after this, the tide began to come in again.

In the morning, long before breakfast, all the children in the bay were down at the beach. The dolphin that had been tethered in the water was dead, and so was the one Mr Lambert had dragged down during the night. The remaining dolphin on the sand and one on the rocks were still breathing. The Lamberts and their friends got a fishing net, and struggled to lift the surviving dolphin from the rocks, but they only tore the net. They tried to grip its tail, its snout, or its fins, but it squirmed so violently that in the end they had to drag it across the rocks by its tail. Even with all this rough handling, the dolphin never once tried to bite them.

Of the seven dolphins they now had only two that might still live, and the one that had spent the night on the sand was the less exhausted of the pair. The other was cut and bruised by the rocks, and couldn't keep upright without assistance from the children. In deep water, it could hardly get up to breathe, but resting on its belly in shallow water it needed only to raise its head an inch or two.

Now the children took over, while the grown-ups got some breakfast ready. And it was entirely due to their devotion, says Mr Lambert, that the two remaining dolphins survived. The water of the early morning in-coming tide was bitterly cold, but the children stayed by the dolphins, guiding them about like model boats and making sure that they could breathe.* After a time the dolphins seemed to be feeling better, and they began to try themselves out again, swimming around without the children's support. Now, of course, there were no whistling sounds from other dolphins to call them back to danger. But they had each other: they always swam toward one another until they met, and then swam side by side, undulating in synchronism, toward the shore again. These

---

* Seven dolphins, seven children, and here are their names: Roddy, Glenis, Peter, Bobby, Pam, Karen, and Gordon. Long lives to them all, and may they always travel safely on the sea!

little outings became longer and more confident, until finally the pair of dolphins simply swam away toward the open sea. 'We stood on the shore and watched, with happiness and sadness all mixed up inside us,' Mr Lambert says. 'We wondered if they would turn back to us again, but they kept on out of sight and we saw them no more.'

◦   ◦   ◦   ◦

By now I have given all the information that is needed to help a stranded dolphin, but here are some useful rules for any others, especially children, who may be in a position to perform a rescue.

The first rule is to remember, once again, that a dolphin is not a fish, and it will not die in a short time simply because it is out of its element. It is not for want of air, but because of its struggles, or because of overheating due to dryness, that it is likely to die. This may take a few hours, so if you are there soon enough, and can arrange to keep its skin moist, you have some time to work in.

The second rule is: do not *drown* a dolphin by putting it into deep water when it is unable to swim. This was the mistake they made at Tryphena with the tethered one; it probably strained at the rope all night until it was exhausted, and then died from drowning. The dolphin Mr Lambert had dragged down in the night was also drowned, as the tide rose over it.

The third rule is that if there are several dolphins stranded together it will be no use removing one or two at a time, unless you can prevent them from hearing the whistling of the others. Remember that they are probably a family or part of a school, and that, whatever caused them to get stranded, their instinct will be telling them above all to keep together. This means you must either get enough helpers to move them all at once, or if that is impossible you can try an experiment that Henry Lambert only thought of after the incident at Tryphena.

With those three rules in mind then, here are some instructions for helping stranded dolphins: Try to find out, first of all, whether they have been stranded long. If they are lively and have no wounds, and their skins are moist, there is no immediate hurry to get them back, so try and get some helpers. Since it takes two people to handle one dolphin, you need twice as many people as there are dolphins. If you cannot get them at once, con-centrate on keeping the dolphins calm, and prevent their skins from drying. When you have your helpers, try to get all the dolphins into deeper water at the same time, mak-ing sure they are able to stay upright and breathe. If they are very exhausted they may be unable to keep upright, even in water that is only a foot or so deep. In that case, support the weaker ones. This is something small children can easily do. If there is strong sunshine, remember that sunburn is very upsetting to dolphins: do not keep the blowhole out of water all the time. As long as you keep its skin wet, the dolphin will feel comfortable, and if it is only barely covered by water it will be able to bend its head up to breathe.

One thing to remember when you handle them: their flippers are the only free-moving limbs they have, and they may not like having them pulled or bent, or even held firm. On the other hand, the flippers and tail flukes are really the only things you can get hold of, and you may simply have to tug them. In any case, there is no need to fear being bitten, because for some reason the gentle dolphin very rarely bites a human being.

But, if you cannot get enough helpers to move the dolphins all at once, you will have the same problem as my friends at Tryphena. In that case it is worth trying Henry Lambert's suggestion. If you were to beach some of the dolphins high and dry (but keep their skins wet!) their signals of distress would not be carried through the water. You might find then that the first ones you took down to the sea would swim off. Then you could take out the remaining dolphins one by one.

On the other hand, the whistlings may have nothing to do with the animals' behaviour. Forrest Wood of Marine Studios is inclined to think not, because he knows of two instances in Florida in which a single stranded animal refused to swim away from the beach when repeatedly moved out to the water, and also because stranded dolphins may be spread along a considerable stretch of beach. 'It does not look as though they try to stay together,' he writes, 'but rather that they are simply strongly impelled to get out of the water.' Someday, perhaps, this mystery, which was also a mystery to Aristotle, will be solved by our further researches into dolphin behaviour. In the meantime, should any of my younger readers succeed in saving some stranded dolphins with the help of these instructions, the cleverest mammals of the land will have helped the cleverest mammals of the sea.

Delphinology

A chronological list of the main contributions to man's understanding of the dolphin, from Aesop to 1960, compiled in part from the References following.

Dates in the classical period are approximate.

600 B.C.   Aesop relates his fable, 'The Monkey and the Dolphin'.

600 B.C.   Arion places in the temple at Tainaron a thank-offering to the dolphin that saved him.

600 B.C.   The legend of Dionysos and the pirates is told in the seventh Homeric Hymn.

540 B.C.   Exekias, in his painting in a famous cup, depicts the legend of Dionysos and the pirates (see Plate 1).

510 B.C.   The city of Taras strikes coins showing a dolphin-rider (see Plate 4).

450 B.C.   Herodotos records the story of Arion.

330 B.C.   In his *History of Animals*, Aristotle accurately describes the dolphin, classing it with the mammals.

320 B.C.   The city of Iasos commemorates a boy-and-dolphin friendship on a coin.

A.D. 70   Pliny the Elder describes the dolphin of the Lucrine Lake, dolphins helping fishermen at Narbonne, dolphins attracted by music, etc., in his *Natural History*.

A.D. 100   Plutarch tells various dolphin stories in his book *On the Cleverness of Animals*, and discusses the intelligence of animals in the sea.

A.D. 109   Pliny the Younger tells the story of the dolphin of Hippo, in a letter.

A.D. 160   Pausanias mentions the dolphin of Poroselene in his *Description of Greece*.

A.D. 200   Oppian discusses at length the character and beneficence of dolphins, the dolphin of Poroselene, Thracian dolphin-hunters, etc., in his *Halieutica*.

A.D. 200   Aelian describes night-fishing with dolphin assistance, in his *On the Characteristics of Animals*.

1551   Pierre Belon accurately depicts the birth of an infant *Tursiops*, with extrusion of placenta, in a woodcut in his *Histoire Naturelle des Estranges Poissons Marins*.

1735   Carl Linnaeus, in his *Systema Naturae*, coins the term and defines the Class Mammalia, includes the cetaceans in it, and gives to the Common Dolphin its name *Delphinus delphis*, a tactful mixture of the Latin and the Greek.

1837   Tom Petrie describes the commensal fishing of dolphins and aboriginals at Moreton Bay, Queensland, in ignorance of the classical precedents.

1887   In New Zealand, William Colenso makes the first collection of classical dolphin tales in his paper, *Ancient Tide-lore and Tales of the Sea from the Two Ends of the World*.

1888   In the year after Colenso made his study, Pelorus Jack is first seen at French Pass.

1904   Pelorus Jack is protected by the New Zealand Government.

1914   L. H. James describes the stillbirth of a porpoise at the Brighton Aquarium, England – the first cetacean birth in captivity, at least in modern times.

1914   C. H. Townsend describes the behaviour of some Bottlenosed Dolphins held captive at the New York Aquarium.

1927   The Linnean Society of London discusses the story of Pelorus Jack at its annual meeting.

1938   W. D. Burden, C. V. Whitney, I. Tolstoy, and others establish Marine Studios at Marineland, Florida.

1940 A. F. McBride's article 'Meet Mr Porpoise', in *Natural History* magazine, gives the first full account of dolphin behaviour based on extensive observations in captivity.

1948 A. F. McBride and D. O. Hebb publish their paper 'Behavior of the Captive Bottle-nose Dolphin, *Tursiops truncatus*' – the first and still the most notable discussion of dolphin intelligence, in relation to that of other 'higher' animals.

1951 A. F. McBride and Henry Kritzler publish their 'Observations on Pregnancy, Parturition' [etc.] – the first observations of dolphin reproduction made under suitable conditions.

1956 His Excellency Sir Willoughby Norrie signs an Order in Council at Wellington, New Zealand, to protect the dolphin Opo at Opononi.

1956 W. E. Schevill and Barbara Lawrence publish 'Food-finding by a Captive Porpoise (*Tursiops truncatus*)' – the first report of echo-location experiments.

1957 Margaret C. Tavolga and F. S. Essapian publish 'The Behavior of the Bottle-nosed dolphin (*Tursiops truncatus*)', in which the mating and birth are now described in very full detail.

1958 W. N. Kellogg publishes his 'Echo-ranging in the Porpoise' – the first conclusive proof.

1959 F. C. Fraser and P. E. Purves describe the anatomy of the cetacean ear to a discussion meeting of the Royal Society in London.

1960 Max O. Kramer reveals the 'dolphins' secret' – his patented discovery of how the dolphin's skin reduces friction drag.

1960 The New Zealand sculptor Russell Clark donates his memorial sculpture of a dolphin with a Maori boy (in Hinuera stone) to the township of Opononi, where local dispute as to a suitable site defers its being erected.

References

~ ~ ~ ~

An asterisk * identifies an item not consulted at first hand;
† indicates a book published too late to be consulted.

Figures in square brackets at end of entries refer to pages
on which the works are quoted or drawn upon.

Classical authors listed in Part II references are fully docu-
mented in Part I below.

Dates of books refer to first publication and not necessarily
to the edition consulted.

PART I

AELIAN, *On the Characteristics of Animals*, tr. A. F. Scholfield
(Loeb Classical Library, Bk. VI, 15). [20–21, 154]

ARISTOTLE, *The History of Animals*, tr. D'Arcy Wentworth
Thompson (Clarendon Press, Oxford, 1910). Book I, 5;
II, 1, 13, 15; III, 1, 7, 20; IV, 8, 9, 10; V, 5; VI, 12;
VIII, 2, 13; IX, 48. [30–31, 42]

ATHENAIOS, *The Deipnosophists*, tr. C. B. Gulick (Loeb Classical
Library, Bk. XIII). [20]

CASE, Josephine Young, 'The Dolphin of the Ancient World',
for the Marineland Research Laboratory (Unpublished,
1958).

COLENSO, William, 'Attested Tales of Dolphins Carrying Men
through the Sea, from Ancient History', in *Ancient Tide-
lore and Tales of the Sea from the Two Ends of the World*
(Hawkes Bay Philosophical Institute, Napier, New
Zealand, 1887). [23]

HEAD, Barclay V., *Historia Numorum: A Manual of Greek
Numismatics* (Clarendon Press, Oxford, 1911). [19]

HERODOTOS, *Histories*, tr. A. D. Godley (Loeb Classical
Library, Bk. I, 23–24).

OPPIAN, *Halieutica*, tr. A. W. Mair (Loeb Classical Library, Bks. I, II, V). [27–43 *passim*]

PAUSANIAS, *Description of Greece*, tr. H. A. Ormerod (Loeb Classical Library, Bk. III: XXV, 7). [27]

PLINY, The Elder, *Natural History*, tr. H. Rackham (Loeb Classical Library, Bk. IX, 7–11). [22–24, 31–33, 37–39]

PLINY, The Younger, *Letters*, tr. William Melmoth, and rev. by W. M. L. Hutchinson (Loeb Classical Library, Bk. IX, 33).

PLUTARCH, 'On the Cleverness of Animals', in *Moralia*, tr. H. Cherniss and W. C. Helmbold (Loeb Classical Library, 975, 979, 984). [16, 22, 42]

SELTMAN, Charles, *Greek Coins* (Methuen, London, 1933).
— *A Book of Greek Coins* (Penguin, London, 1953).

STEBBINS, Eunice Burr, *The Dolphin in the Literature and Art of Greece and Rome** (George Banta, Wisconsin, 1929).

THOMPSON, Sir D'Arcy Wentworth, *ΔΕΛΦΙΣ*. Article in *A Glossary of Greek Fishes* (Oxford University Press, 1947).

WAGNER, R., 'Delphin'. Article in Pauly-Wissowa, *Real-Encyclopädie der classischen Altertumswissenschaft*, vol. 4, col. 2504–2510. (Stuttgart.) Gives an exhaustive list of references to the dolphin in classical literature. [14–16]

XENOPHON, *Anabasis*, tr. C. L. Brownson (Loeb Classical Library, Bk. V, 4, 28). [40]

PART II

AELIAN, *On the Characteristics of Animals*, Bk. II, 8. [153]

AESOP, 'The Monkey and the Dolphin', in *An Anthology of Fables* (Dent, Everyman's Library, London, 1913). [112]

ANDERSON, John, *Account of the Zoological Results of Two Expeditions to Western Yunnan (1879)*.* Quoted in Norman and Fraser (*q.v.* below). [167]

ANONYMOUS, 'Saved by a Porpoise' (a letter). *Natural History*, 58 (11), pp. 385–386 (1949). [113]

ARISTOTLE, *The History of Animals*. [61, 134, 139–143]

BACKHOUSE, Kenneth, 'Locomotion and Direction-finding in Whales and Dolphins', *New Scientist*, vol. 7, no. 164, pp. 26–28 (1960). [62]

BEDDARD, F. E., *A Book of Whales* (John Murray, London, 1900). [77, 162]

BELON, Pierre, *Histoire Naturelle des Estranges Poissons Marins* (1551).* Cited in Singer (*q.v.* below). [238]

BINGLEY, Reverend W., *Animal Biography, or Authentic Anecdotes of the Lives, Manner, and Economy of the Animal Creation* (London, 1802). [139n.]

BOURLIÈRE, François, *The Natural History of Mammals*, tr. H. M. Parshley (Harrap, London, 1955). [71–72, 94]

BROWN, David H., and NORRIS, Kenneth S., 'Observations of Captive and Wild Cetaceans', *Journal of Mammalogy*, vol. 37, pp. 311–323 (1956). [109–111]

CALDWELL, D. K., 'Evidence of Home-Range of an Atlantic Bottle-nose Dolphin', *Journal of Mammalogy*, vol. 36, pp. 304–305 (1955).

DAKIN, W. J., *Whalemen Adventurers: The Story of Whaling in Australian Waters* (Angus and Robertson, Sydney, 1934), pp. 134–136. [169 ff.]

DIJKGRAFF, S., 'Hearing in Bony Fishes', *Proceedings of the Royal Society*, series B, vol. 152, pp. 51–54 (1960).

ESSAPIAN, Frank S., 'The Birth and Growth of a Porpoise', *Natural History*, 62 (9), pp. 392–399 (1953). [97–98]

— 'A Common Dolphin – Uncommonly Marked', *Everglades Natural History*, vol. 2, no. 4 (1954).

— 'Speed-induced Skinfolds in the Bottle-nosed Porpoise, *Tursiops truncatus*', *Breviora*, no. 43 (1955). [65–66]

—, and TAVOLGA, Margaret C. (1957). *See* under Tavolga below.

EWER, R. F., *Whales* (Penguin New Biology No. 2, London, 1947). [71]

FEJER, A. A., and BACKUS, R. H., 'Porpoises and the Bow-riding of Ships under Way', *Nature*, vol. 188, pp. 700–703 (1960). [68–70]

FERMOR, Patrick Leigh, *Mani: Travels in the Southern Peloponnese* (John Murray, London, 1958). [51–52]

FRASER, F. C., 'Sound Emitted by Dolphins', *Nature*, vol. 160, p. 759 (1947).

— 'Some Aquatic Adaptations of Whales and Dolphins',* *Proceedings of the Royal Institution*, vol. 37, p. 167 (1959).

—, and NORMAN, J. R. (1937), *see* under Norman below.

—, and PURVES, P. E., 'Hearing in Whales', *Endeavour*, vol. 18 (70), pp. 93–98 (1959). [133–135]

—, 'Anatomy and Function of the Cetacean Ear', *Proceedings of the Royal Society*, Series B, vol. 152, pp. 62–77 (1960). [133–135]

GAWN, R. W. L., 'Aspects of the Locomotion of Whales', *Nature*, vol. 161, pp. 44–46 (1948).

GRAY, Sir James, 'Studies in Animal Locomotion', *Journal of Experimental Biology*, vol. 13, pp. 192–199 (1936).

— 'Aspects of the Locomotion of Whales', *Nature*, vol. 161, pp. 199–200 (1948). [63]

— *How Animals Move*. The Royal Institution Christmas Lectures, 1951 (Cambridge University Press, 1953). [63, 73]

HALDANE, J. B. S., 'On Being the Right Size' (essay), in *Possible Worlds* (Chatto and Windus, London, 1927). [76]

HARDY, Sir Alister, *The Open Sea*, Part II, 'Fish & Fisheries'. (Collins, New Naturalist Series, London, 1959). [177]

— 'Was Man More Aquatic in the Past?' *New Scientist*, vol. 7, no. 174, pp. 642–645 (1960).

— 'Will Man Be More Aquatic in the Future?' *New Scientist*, vol. 7, no. 175, pp. 730–733 (1960).

HAYES, W. D., 'Wave-riding of Dolphins', *Nature*, vol. 172, p. 1060 (1953). [67–68]

— 'Wave-riding Dolphins', *Science*, vol. 130, pp. 1657–1658 (1959). [67–68]

HAYTER, Adrian, *Sheila in the Wind* (Hodder and Stoughton, London, 1959). [82]

HEBB, D. O. (1948), *see* under McBride below.

HILL, Ralph Nading, *Window in the Sea* (an account of the founding and operation of Marine Studios in Florida) (Gollancz, London, 1956).

HUBBS, Carl L., 'Dolphin Protecting Dead Young', *Journal of Mammalogy*, vol. 34, p. 498 (1953). [114]

IRVING, L., SCHOLANDER, P. F., and GRINNELL, S. W., 'The Respiration of the Porpoise, *Tursiops truncatus*',* *Journal of Cellular and Comparative Physiology*, vol. 17, pp. 145–168. (1941) Quoted in Bourlière (*q.v.* above).

JAMES, L. H., 'Birth of a Porpoise at the Brighton Aquarium',* *Proceedings of the Zoological Society*, pp. 1061–1062 (London, 1914). Quoted in Tavolga and Essapian. [83*n*.]

KELLOGG, Remington, 'Whales, Giants of the Sea' (with 31 paintings by Else Bostelmann of the better-known species of cetacea), *National Geographic Magazine*, vol. 77 (1), pp. 35–90 (1940).

KELLOGG, W. N., and KOHLER, Robert, 'Reactions of the Porpoise to Ultrasonic Frequencies', *Science*, vol. 116, pp. 250–252 (1952). [128]

—, —, and MORRIS, H. N., 'Porpoise Sounds as Sonar Signals', *Science*, vol. 117, pp. 239–243 (1953). [128]

— *Sounds of Sea Animals*, an LP record with commentary, containing sounds made by dolphins, alone and in schools; at normal and reduced speeds, showing sonar effect (Folkways Records, FPX 125, 1955).

— 'Echo-ranging in the Porpoise' ['Perception of objects by reflected sound is demonstrated for the first time in marine animals'], *Science*, vol. 128, pp. 982–988 (1958). [128 ff.]

— 'Auditory Perception of Submerged Objects by Porpoises', *Journal of the Acoustical Society of America*, vol. 31 (1), pp. 1–6 (1959). [129]

— 'Size Discrimination by Reflected Sound in a Bottle-nose Porpoise', *Journal of Comparative and Physiological Psychology*, vol. 52 (5), pp. 509–514 (1959). [130]

— 'Auditory Scanning in the Dolphin', *Psychological Record*, vol. 10, pp. 25–27 (1960).—*Porpoises and Sonar* † (Chicago University Press, 1961). [131]

KRAMER, Max O., 'The Dolphins' Secret', *New Scientist*, vol. 7, (183), pp. 1118–1120 (1960). [64–66]

KRITZLER, Henry, 'Observations on the Pilot Whale in Captivity', *Journal of Mammalogy*, vol. 33, pp. 321–334 (1952).

KULLENBERG, B., 'Sound Emitted by Dolphins', *Nature*, vol. 160, p. 648 (1947). [82 ff.]

LA GORCE, G. G., 'Marineland, Florida's Giant Fish Bowl', *National Geographic Magazine*, vol. 102 (5), pp. 679–694 (1952).

LAMB, F. Bruce, 'The Fisherman's Porpoise', *Natural History*, vol. 63 (5), pp. 231–232 (1954). [164–166]

LAWRENCE, Barbara, and SCHEVILL, W. E., 'Tursiops as an Experimental Subject', *Journal of Mammalogy*, vol. 35, pp. 225–232 (1954).

LILLY, J. C., 'Some Considerations Regarding Basic Mechanisms of Positive and Negative Types of Motivation', *American Journal of Psychiatry*, vol. 115, pp. 498–504 (1958). [105–107]

— *Man and Dolphin†* (Gollancz, London, 1962).

LONGMAN, Heber A., 'New Records of Cetacea – Aboriginals and Porpoises', *Memoirs of the Queensland Museum*, vol. VIII, pp. 275 ff. (1926). [159–161]

LORENZ, Konrad, *Man Meets Dog*, tr. Marjorie Kerr Wilson (Methuen, London, 1954). [178*n*.]

MCBRIDE, Arthur F., 'Meet Mr Porpoise', *Natural History*, vol. 45, pp. 16–29 (1940). [124]

— 'Evidence for Echolocation by Cetaceans' [notes published posthumously], *Deep-Sea Research*, vol. 3, pp. 153–154 (1956). The notes were written in 1947.

—, and HEBB, D. O., 'Behavior of the Captive Bottle-nose Dolphin, *Tursiops truncatus*', *Journal of Comparative and Physiological Psychology*, vol. 41 (2), pp. 111–123 (1948). [102–103, 107–108]

—, and KRITZLER, Henry, 'Observations on Pregnancy, Parturition, and Post-natal Behaviour in the Bottlenose Dolphin', *Journal of Mammalogy*, vol. 32 (3), pp. 251–266 (1951). [96–101]

MATTHEWS, L. Harrison, 'The Swimming of Dolphins' [reply to Woodcock, *q.v.* below], *Nature*, vol. 161, p. 731 (1948).

— *British Mammals* (Collins, New Naturalist series, London, 1952). [72]

MELVILLE, Herman, *Moby Dick, or the White Whale* (Harper, New York, 1851), chapter XXXII, 'Cetology'. [51]

MOORE, J. C., 'Bottlenosed Dolphins Support Remains of Young', *Journal of Mammalogy*, vol. 36, pp. 466–467 (1955). [142*n*.]

NORMAN, J. R., and FRASER, F. C., *Giant Fishes, Whales, and Dolphins* (Putnam, London, 1937). [47, 162–163]

O BRIEN, Conor, *Across Three Oceans* (Rupert Hart-Davis, The Mariner's Library, London, 1951), pp. 240–241. [144–145]

OPPIAN, *Halieutica*. [47, 89, 221]

PARRY, D. A., 'Aspects of the Locomotion of Whales', *Nature*, vol. 161, p. 200 (1948).

— 'The Swimming of Whales', *Journal of Experimental Biology*, vol. 26, pp. 24–34 (1949). [63]

PLINY, The Elder, *Natural History*. [49, 134, 146]

PLINY, The Younger, *Letters*. [148]

PLUTARCH, *On the Cleverness of Animals*. [117*n*., 148–149]

PURVES, P. E., 'Measuring the Age of Whales', *New Scientist*, vol. 7, no. 179, pp. 1008–1009 (1960).

REYSENBACH DE HAAN, F. W., 'Some Aspects of Mammalian Hearing Under Water', *Proceedings of the Royal Society*, series B, no. 152, pp. 54–61 (1960). [134]

RYDER, M. L., 'The Dolphin's Secret' [a letter enlarging upon Kramer; *see* above], *New Scientist*, vol. 8 no. 195, p. 424 (1960).

SANDERSON, Ivan T., *Follow the Whale* (Cassell, London, 1958). [142, 144, 163]

SCHEVILL, William E., and LAWRENCE, Barbara, 'Auditory Response of a Bottle-nosed Porpoise, *Tursiops truncatus*, to Frequencies above 100 *kc*', *Journal of Experimental Zoology*, vol. 124, no. 1 (1953).

SCHEVILL, William E., 'Food-finding by a Captive Porpoise (*Tursiops truncatus*)', *Breviora*, vol. 53, pp. 1–15 (1956). [125 ff.]

SCHOLANDER, P. F., 'Wave-riding Dolphins: How Do They Do It?', *Science*, vol. 129, pp. 1085–1087, and vol. 130, p. 1658 (1959). [67–68]

SERGEANT, D. E., 'Age Determination in Odontocete Whales from Dentinal Growth Layers', *Norwegian Whaling Gazette*, vol. 6, pp. 273–288 (1959). [94]

SIEBNALER, J. B., and CALDWELL, D. K., 'Cooperation among Adult Dolphins', *Journal of Mammalogy*, vol. 37, pp. 126–128 (1956). [114]

SINGER, Charles, *A History of Biology* (Clarendon Press, Oxford, 1931). [140n.]

TAVOLGA, Margaret C., and ESSAPIAN, Frank S., 'The Behavior of the Bottle-nosed Dolphin (*Tursiops truncatus*): Mating, Pregnancy, Parturition, and Mother-Infant Behavior', *Zoologica*, vol. 42, no. 1, pp. 11–31 (1957).

TOWNSEND, C. H., 'The Porpoise in Captivity', *Zoologica*, vol. 1, no. 16, pp. 289–299 (1914). [148n.]

VIGOUREUX, P., 'Underwater Sound', *Proceedings of the Royal Society*, series B, vol. 152, pp. 49–51 (1960). [134]

WOOD, Forrest G., Jr, *Porpoise Sounds*. A Gramophone Record of Underwater Sounds Made by *Tursiops truncatus* and *Stenella plagiodon** (Marineland Research Laboratory, 1952).

— 'Underwater Sound Production and Concurrent Behavior of Captive Porpoises, *Tursiops truncatus* and *Stenella plagiodon*', *Bulletin of Marine Science of the Gulf and Carribbean*, vol. 3, pp. 120–133 (1953).

— 'Porpoise Play', *Mariner* [mimeographed house organ of Marine Studios], March 1954, p. 4. [100]

WOODCOCK, Alfred H., 'The Swimming of Dolphins' ['motionless' swimming near a ship's bow], *Nature*, vol. 161, p. 602 (1948). [66]

—, and McBRIDE, A. F., 'Wave-riding of Dolphins', *Journal of Experimental Biology*, vol. 28, p. 215 (1951). [67]

YOUNG, J. Z., *The Life of Vertebrates* (Clarendon Press, Oxford, 1950).

PART III

ANONYMOUS, 'Pelorus Jack', *The New Zealand School Journal*, Part 3, vol. 1, no. 1 (1907).

BEST, Elsdon, 'Tuhoe: Children of the Mist', *Polynesian Society Memoirs*, vol. 6 (1925). [184, 188–189]

CHAMBERLAIN, Venus, Scrapbook of Articles, Postcards, News Clippings, etc., on Pelorus Jack. Photocopy now in Turnbull Library, Wellington (1910–59). [190 ff.]

COWAN, James, *Pelorus Jack: The White Dolphin of French Pass . . . with Maori Legends* (Whitcombe and Tombs, Christchurch, 1911).

GREY, Sir George, *Polynesian Mythology and Ancient Traditional History of the New Zealanders, As Furnished by Their Chiefs and Priests* (John Murray, London, 1855). [186–187]

GRIMBLE, Sir Arthur, *A Pattern of Islands* (John Murray, London, 1952).

MARINE DEPARTMENT, New Zealand, 'Pelorus Jack, Protection of', File No. 2/12/34. Photocopy now in Alexander Turnbull Library, Wellington (1903–59). [196 ff.]

NEW ZEALAND NATIONAL FILM UNIT, Pictorial Parade No. 47 contains a few feet of film clearly showing Pelorus Jack leaping ahead of a ship, and passengers watching; and a longer film of the Opononi dolphin playing with Jill Baker, being scratched with an oar, and tossing a beachball and a beer bottle (New Zealand National Film Library catalogue No. A 2166, 1956).

TOI, Piwai, 'Opo the Gay Dolphin', *Te Ao Hou* ['The New World'],vol. 6, no. 3, pp. 22–24 (Wellington, 1958). [209 ff.]

TWAIN, Mark, *Following the Equator: A Journey round the World* (Harper, New York, 1897).

WEBBER, G. W., 'Pelorus Jack: Was He a Risso's Dolphin?', *Weekly News* (Auckland), April 29, 1953. [192]

WILSON, C. A., *Legends and Mysteries of the Maori* (Harrap, London, 1932). [184, 185]

Index

⋄ ⋄ ⋄ ⋄

DATES of classical writers mentioned, and scientific names of fish and cetacea, etc., are given in this index.